curtains
DRAPERIES & SHADES

By Carol Spier and the Editors of Sunset Books

Menlo Park, California

SUNSET BOOKS

Vice President, General Manager: Richard A. Smeby
Vice President, Editorial Director: Bob Doyle
Director of Operations: Rosann Sutherland
Marketing Manager: Linda Barker
Art Director: Vasken Guiragossian
Special Sales: Brad Moses

CURTAINS, DRAPERIES & SHADES was produced
in conjunction with Melnick & Meyer Books, Inc.
Directors: Marsha Melnick, Susan E. Meyer

STAFF FOR THIS BOOK

Editor: Carol Spier
Book Design: Areta Buk/Thumb Print
Illustration: Beverly Bozarth Colgan, Celia M. Mitchell, and Dartmouth Publishing, Inc.
Materials Photography: Tom Haynes. Other photography credits are on page 144.
Prepress Coordinator: Eligio Hernández
Production Specialist: Linda M. Bouchard

COVER: Softly striped floor-length rod-pocket curtains complete the simple elegance of this formal dining area. Interior design by Paulette Trainor. Cover design by Vasken Guiragossian. Photography by E. Andrew McKinney.

10 9 8 7 6 5 4 3 2 1
First Printing June 2007
Copyright © 2007, Sunset Publishing Corporation, Menlo Park, CA 94025. Fourth edition.
All rights reserved, including the right of reproduction in whole or in part in any form.
ISBN-13: 978-0-376-01740-6
ISBN-10: 0-376-01740-6
Library of Congress Control Number: 2007923288
Printed in the United States of America

For additional copies of *Curtains, Draperies & Shades* or any other Sunset book,
visit us at *www.sunsetbooks.com* or call 1-800-526-5111.

contents

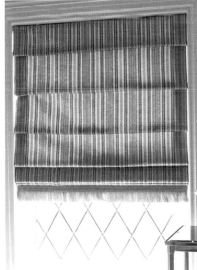

getting started

BUYING FABRIC and sewing the project may be the most pleasurable part of making a window treatment, but the planning process is where the real work is done. It's the key to a successful project.

It's a good idea to understand your options for various styles of windows and become familiar with the basics of how color, pattern, and texture affect the overall look. Take time to find the style that is right for you, look at fabric samples in your home at different times of the day and at night, and think about your lifestyle and design preferences before you begin.

a look at window treatments

IF YOU'RE TIRED of staring at a bare or poorly dressed window, it's hard to resist the urge to buy some fabric, set up the machine, and start sewing. But, like any project, a successful window treatment relies on some thoughtful decision making.

First, become familiar with the various styles and terms so you'll know how to tell a curtain from a drapery and a valance from a cornice. Then, let an awareness of your functional and decorative needs, as well as your personal style, guide you in choosing the treatment that's right for you.

coming to terms

If you haven't kept up with window treatment fashions, you're in for a pleasant surprise. Familiar styles have been joined by a collection of innovative top treatments, from casual valances to classic swags and cascades. Here's a brief look at your options.

CURTAINS. By definition, curtains are gathered on a rod or attached to a rod by tabs, ties, or rings. If the curtains open and close, it's by hand.

In general, length sets the style with curtains. Café curtains cover only the lower half of the window, ending at the sill or apron. With cafés, use a generous amount of fabric so they don't look skimpy.

Full-length curtains lend themselves to both elegant and informal schemes. Curtains that are tied in poufs called bishop's sleeves and curtains that puddle on the floor impart a luxurious mood; in contrast, simple floor-length curtains tied back above the sash create a casual effect.

Curtains combine well with other treatments. If you like the look of stationary curtain panels but you want some privacy, pair the curtains with miniblinds or a pleated shade. For a more finished effect, top them with a cornice or valance.

DRAPERIES. Long considered staid and predictable, today's draperies offer a variety of intriguing pleat styles and decorative hardware.

Draperies have pleated headings that attach to rods by means of drapery hooks. They are opened and closed either by hand or by a traverse rod system.

Pinch pleats, the traditional drapery heading, consist of three shallow folds tacked together several inches below the top edge. Variations include goblet, reverse pinch, and butterfly pleats. Pencil pleats are achieved with the use of shirring tape sewn to the back of the drapery heading.

Though most draperies that are hung on conventional or decorative rods are meant to be opened and closed, drapery panels can also be stationary. Pleated side panels tie back beautifully because the pleats fall in consistent folds.

SHADES. Shades offer an enormous array of versatile and different-looking styles. Moreover, shades are as hardworking as they are good-looking, ensuring privacy, controlling light, and conserving energy.

Roman, balloon, and cloud shades all raise and lower by means of cords threaded through rings sewn to the back of the shade. From the front of a flat Roman shade, you see crisp, tailored folds. A variation, called a soft-fold Roman shade, has extra length in the folds and falls in horizontal pleats even when it's lowered.

Vertical pleats in balloon shades create poufs at the lower edge. The shirring at the top of a cloud shade adds softness that poufs at the hem.

Because they're easy to make, roller shades are popular in informal areas and in children's rooms. Top them with a valance or cornice or use them for privacy under held-back panels.

OPPOSITE: *Tucks sewn across the top of sheer curtains create linear shadows as the light filters through, adding an interesting finish to a simple window treatment.*

TOP: *Shaped rods can be custom-made for bow and bay windows. Here elegant cut velvet draperies, hanging on rings, are a lovely complement to the faux-finished walls.*

BOTTOM: *This curtain and companion Roman shade, both with coordinating borders, have a tailored yet informal look. The shade keeps the small alcove more open than a second curtain would.*

a look at window treatments

VALANCES. Some valances, such as rod-pocket, Roman, and balloon, look like short versions of their longer counterparts. Others are more innovative, sporting shaped, poufed, or rolled lower edges.

Used alone, valances bring a whisper of style and color to windows. Placed over another treatment, they not only conceal the heading but also lend a decorative flourish. Arched, tapered, or scalloped valances crown curtains and draperies, adding flowing lines and visual interest. Box-pleated valances provide a classic top treatment for tailored draperies. In children's rooms, a skirt or stagecoach valance can dress up a blind or roller shade.

The lower edges of valances offer unlimited possibilities for trimmings, from ruffles and piping to contrast banding and fringe.

CORNICES. Because their edges are so delineated, cornices add architectural interest. The effect depends, in part, on the shape of the lower edge; a straight edge is simple and tailored; one with scallops is more formal.

When used on more than one window in a room, cornices unify the space and create a pleasing visual rhythm. They also display the fabric's design over a flat area.

In addition, cornices serve two very practical purposes: they cover the heading and hardware at the top of the undertreatment, and they block cold drafts coming from the window.

SWAGS AND CASCADES. Among the most impressive of all window treatments, swags and cascades bring distinction and classic form to windows. Once found in only the most opulent settings, today's versions can be more casual and adapt to informal decorating schemes as well.

Challenging to make and mount, traditional and cutout swags look like flowing lengths of fabric. They're often accompanied by cascades. For a more formal look, put swags and cascades over long side panels or on top of sheers.

Easy-to-make running swags can be wrapped around a pole, draped in decorative swag holders, or held in place with knots or tabs.

TOP LEFT: *This grandly proportioned swagged Roman valance over panels is a soft contrast to a flat sloped ceiling.*

BOTTOM LEFT: *Here a delicate painted cornice with a gathered skirt over panels echoes the design of the bed hangings.*

OPPOSITE: *Traditional swags made in muslin look sweet when topped with a valance made of a tiny double ruffle.*

the role of a window

Windows are designed to admit light and air and allow in views of the outside world. But windows and their treatments play a myriad of other roles, ranging from functional to purely decorative.

LIGHT. The primary function of windows is to provide natural light. How much light actually enters the room depends on your window treatment choice. To admit the maximum amount of light into the room, choose a treatment that stacks back completely. To filter light, choose sheers, laces, and casement fabrics. To block the light, select curtains, draperies, and shades lined with blackout linings.

CLIMATE. To take advantage of refreshing breezes, choose treatments that completely clear the window. Heavy fabrics block the flow of air more than lightweight ones. Most window treatments have an insulating effect, because they inhibit air from circulating.

PRIVACY. Any window in your home has the potential for allowing people to see inside. Sheers and lightweight fabrics let in some light during the day while providing privacy, but you'll need a heavier window covering that closes completely for total privacy.

NOISE CONTROL. Window treatments can reduce noise from both outside and inside the house. In general, the softer and more generous the treatment, the more sound it will absorb.

VIEW. When the view deserves to be seen, either choose a fabric that repeats the color and pattern on the wall so as not to distract the eye from the view beyond or choose a treatment that frames the window like a work of art. When the view is unattractive, select bold patterns and colors so that the window treatment itself attracts attention, or obscure the view with sheer or semisheer fabrics.

color, pattern, and texture

A WELL-PLANNED window treatment combines the basic design elements of color, pattern, and texture with subtle design concepts to create a beautiful, balanced effect.

color

No matter which window treatment you prefer, your first decisions will be about color. The following tips will help you choose and combine colors:

❑ To develop a color sense, look through decorating magazines and books and pull or mark examples of fabrics, window treatments, and rooms that appeal to you. Though they may seem unrelated at first, you'll gradually see a pattern to your preferences.

❑ Take your color cues from colors you and other members of the household love in nature, in fashion, and in interiors.

❑ If you want to create more visual space or a background for other interesting items in a room, choose a color for your window treatment that matches or is a similar value to the wall color. If you want to create interest and take your eye away from other elements in a room, choose a contrasting color from the wall color.

❑ Low value, less-intense colors may "wear" better visually than strong ones.

❑ Color changes with the lighting. Purchase a yard of the fabric that you are considering, tape it to the wall, and look at it throughout the day and by artificial light at night.

❏ The impact of color is intensified when it's used in large quantities. A very bright color may be better used as an accent pillow or a simple valance or swag than as a full-length window treatment.

❏ Color is affected by the direction of light. Windows facing south and east let in warm, cheery light. Indirect northern light is softer and cooler, and light from the west is harshest of all.

pattern

Pattern enriches all types of decorating schemes, adding depth, movement, and visual interest. The following tips on using and combining pattern will help you gain pattern confidence.

❏ Patterns that share at least one color combine easily.

❏ The size of the pattern should correspond to the scale of the room and its windows. Small-scale patterns are often used in cozy rooms. Large-scale patterns create the impression that a room is smaller than it actually is, so may be better shown in spacious rooms.

❏ Similar patterns of different scales also combine well, such as small checks and larger plaids.

ABOVE: *Contrast fabric inside the pleats adds subtle pizzazz to these kick-pleat valances—a nice touch in a room where blocks of vivid color play a starring role.*

OPPOSITE TOP: *One richly patterned fabric may be all that's needed to enliven a basic design—as here on an upholstered straight cornice with a self-fabric welt along the lower edge and the matching panels beneath it.*

OPPOSITE BOTTOM: *Companion fabrics make it easier to pull off complex designs, as on these pinch-pleat valances and cuffed draperies, where a large floral pairs with a small lattice used for triangle overlays and hem bands.*

color, pattern, and texture

❑ Pattern combinations can be simple, such as the unpatterned windows, walls, and furnishings seen in the clean Shaker style as well as in more formal schemes. Another approach is to use pattern throughout—on the windows, on the walls, even on the furnishings. This all-out mix of patterns, reminiscent of Victorian times, can be tricky to pull off. A more doable strategy is to combine pattern with plain color for a balanced look. Keeping walls plain while dressing windows in pattern draws attention to the window and the window treatment.

❑ Consider how a pattern will appear placed on different surfaces. A full-length gathered or pleated window treatment will look entirely different from a flat Roman shade, even when the same fabric is used for both.

❑ Avoid combining too many patterns in one area. A good rule of thumb is to use one bold pattern on a large surface so that it predominates. Then add two or possibly three smaller-scale patterns, distributing them around the room in order to avoid pattern clusters.

texture

Shimmering faille, nubby woven wool, and tasseled fringe—all window treatment materials possess texture, from distinctive to subtle.

When the texture is smooth, light is reflected and colors appear lighter and more lustrous, and often a bit formal.

When there's more texture, fabric appears duller because the light is absorbed rather than reflected. Noticeably textured fabrics tend to be casual.

A monochromatic color scheme with very little pattern allows for more texture than a scheme with bold color and pattern. For a beautiful blend of rough and smooth surfaces throughout a room, try to introduce enough texture to create interest, but not so much that visual chaos results.

ABOVE: *This striking set of Roman shades, with a perfectly centered motif repeated on each, demonstrates how good planning pays off when you are working with large patterns.*

OPPOSITE: *Light, airy fabric makes these traditional swags with cascades and jabots anything but ponderous. They're bias cut, have bound edges, and are mounted in a bay window above simple café curtains with small headings.*

window math

THE KEY TO making treatments that fit your windows perfectly is careful measuring and calculating. This is a critical job—a miscalculation of even an inch or two could leave you short yards of fabric. The instructions in this section will guide you.

Read the following sequence to get a feel for the entire process involved in making window treatments. Then you will be ready to measure your window and determine the yardage needed for your project.

Choose your window treatment project and the fabric from which to make it (projects begin on page 30; fabric guidelines are on pages 21–26).

Decide on the type of hardware you'll use (for hardware information on your particular treatment, look at the beginning of each project chapter). Purchase the hardware after you've measured your windows, but don't install it until after your project is completed.

Measure your windows according to the instructions that follow, and record the measurements in the spaces provided in the window diagram (right). Guidelines are included to help you determine how much coverage you need above, below, and on the sides of the window.

Fill in the window treatment work sheet on page 16 to determine the yardage required. (The work sheet applies to all treatments except swags and cornices; you'll find measuring and calculating instructions for those treatments in the project section.) Fill in every box that applies; put a slash through those that don't.

Purchase the fabric and any trimmings and notions.

Make the window treatment, mark its placement on the window, and then install the hardware and treatment.

the professional approach to measuring

This approach, used by professionals, works from the window measurements rather than from the hardware.

TAKING WINDOW MEASUREMENTS

Measuring a window opening is straightforward (see drawing below). Be sure to use a steel tape measure and write in the spaces provided.

If your treatment will be mounted inside the window, you need measure only the width of the opening (A) and the length (B). But if your window treatment will hang outside the opening, as most do, you'll have to determine not only the width and length of the opening but also the area to be covered to the left (C) and right (D) of the opening and from the top (E) and bottom (F).

Side extensions depend on how much light control and privacy you want (see page 9). For treatments that don't clear the glass completely when opened, extensions can range from 2 to 10 inches. For draperies that pull all the way off the window, see the next page for stackback information.

Shades usually extend $\frac{1}{2}$ inch beyond the trim board on each side or 2 inches beyond the window opening if there's no trim. If treatments are being teamed, the extensions must be sufficient to allow the top treatment hardware to clear the undertreatment.

The top of a window treatment is often even with the top of the trim board; other options are just below the ceiling, at the bottom of crown molding, or halfway between the ceiling and window opening. Valances typically begin 8 inches above the window opening.

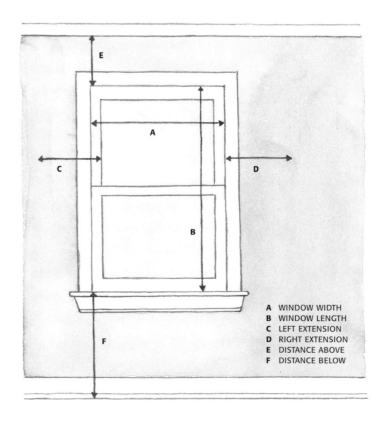

A WINDOW WIDTH
B WINDOW LENGTH
C LEFT EXTENSION
D RIGHT EXTENSION
E DISTANCE ABOVE
F DISTANCE BELOW

Treatments are generally most pleasing when they end in line with either the window or floor. Floor-length treatments should end ¹/₂ inch short of the floor. There are two exceptions: If you use an open-weave fabric or live in a particularly humid area, end the treatment 1 inch above the floor. In double treatments, the inner treatment should be ¹/₂ inch shorter than the outer one.

USING EXISTING HARDWARE

If the hardware already on your windows is in good condition and meets your needs, you can reuse it. Take the following measurements and use them to fill in the window treatment work sheet on page 16.

1 Measure the rod or pole from end to end for the rod or pole size.

2 Measure from the front of the hardware to the wall for the return. For draperies, measure the center overlap when the treatment is closed.

3 *For rod-pocket curtains or valances,* measure from the top of the rod or pole to where the treatment will end; add the depth of the heading, if used. Add take-up allowance (see page 17, step 7). To ensure correct length, pin the hem and check it before stitching.

For tab curtains (see page 46), the measurements depend on tab length.

For draperies on a standard traverse rod, measure from the top of rod to the floor; subtract ¹/₂ inch. *For draperies on a decorative rod,* measure from the bottom of the rod or rings to the floor. *For curtains on rings,* measure from the bottom of the rings to where the treatment will end.

puddling

A designer option, puddling is a dramatic pool of extra fabric at the hem of floor-length draperies and curtains. For the right look, add 10 to 12 inches to the length and use crisp fabrics such as silk douppioni or linen.

allowing for stackback

Curtains or draperies that open to expose the entire glass area—or most of it—need room to stack beyond the glass. This area is called the stackback.

For most fabrics you'll need to allow one-third the width of the glass area (or the area you wish to expose) for the stackback. For a two-way draw treatment, place half the stackback on each side of the glass. For a one-way draw, the entire stackback goes on one side.

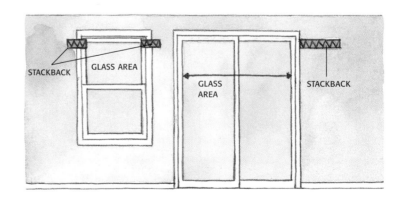

window treatment work sheet

NUMBER OF WIDTHS

Left Extension	Window Width	Right Extension	Rod, Pole, or Board Size	Return + Overlap* + Return	Finished Width	Fullness	Side Hems	Total Width Required	Usable Fabric Width	Number of Widths
+	+	=	+	=	x		+	=	÷	=

*FOR DRAPERIES ONLY

TOTAL YARDS

Distance Above	Window Length	Distance Below	Finished Length	Top Allowance	Hem	1" Ravel Allowance	Cut Length or Repeat Cut Length	Number of Widths	Required Fabric in Inches	Inches Converted to Yards	Yards Needed
+	+	=	+	+	+	=	x	=	÷ 36	=	

LINING

Finished Length* + 5"*	Number of Widths	Inches Converted to Yards	Yards Needed
x	÷ 36	=	

*FOR CURTAINS AND DRAPERIES ONLY; FOR OTHER TREATMENTS, SEE INDIVIDUAL PROJECTS.

RETURN SIZE CHART

Treatments on Window	Return Size*
1 Treatment	$3\frac{1}{2}$"
2 Treatments	$5\frac{1}{2}$"
3 Treatments	$7\frac{1}{2}$"

*MAY VARY; CHECK MANUFACTURER'S INSTRUCTIONS.

yardage calculations

Though the process may seem laborious, only careful calculating will ensure that you'll have sufficient fabric to complete your project. Using the window measurements you just made, follow the steps below, filling in the window treatment sheet as you go.

To determine allowances for fullness, hems, headings, and pockets, turn to the project you're making (see the projects section beginning on page 31) and look under "Calculating Yardage."

DETERMINING NUMBER OF WIDTHS

Number of widths is determined by adding amounts needed for side hems and fullness to the finished width of the treatment as it will hang, closed, at the window.

1 Add left extension, width of window opening, and right extension to get rod, pole, or board size.

2 To that figure, add returns—the distance from front of hardware to wall—and the overlap.

For return size for one or more treatments on a single window, see the chart above. For traversing draperies only, add $1\frac{1}{2}$ inches to each panel for the overlap.

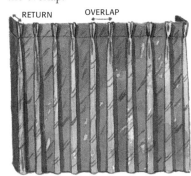

RETURN   OVERLAP

3 Multiply finished width by desired fullness, usually 2½ times for medium-weight fabrics and 3 times for sheers.

4 Add the side hem allowances for the total width required.

5 Divide total width by fabric width to arrive at number of widths needed. Most fabrics and linings are 48 to 54 inches wide. If lining is different than fabric, calculate number of lining widths separately.

Sheers, often 118 inches wide, are meant to be fabricated without seams, with selvages running parallel to floor. This is called "railroading." In this case, divide total width by 36 inches for yardage.

6 If number of widths determined in step 5 isn't a whole number, round it off. For any treatment with horizontal fullness, round off to the next whole number if the fractional part is ½ or greater (for example, 3.7 widths rounds off to 4); round off to the smaller whole number if the fractional part is less than ½. If your number is 1 plus any fraction, round up to 2; otherwise, you would split one width.

Most curtains and draperies open at center; each half of the treatment is called a panel. When you have two panels, divide the total number of fabric widths in half to determine how many widths make up each panel. For example, a pair of draperies that requires 5 widths of fabric will have 2½ widths in each panel. With draperies, never use less than half a width (anything narrower is difficult to pleat).

For Roman or roller shades, always round up to the next full width.

DETERMINING YARDAGE FOR UNPATTERNED FABRIC

Total yardage is based on cut length (the finished length plus headings, hems, and a ravel allowance) multiplied by the number of widths. See below for information on how to calculate cut length and total yardage for patterned fabric.

Continue on the second line of the work sheet.

7 Add length of window opening to distance above and below opening to arrive at finished length.

For curtains on flat rods, add ½ inch to finished length to allow for take-up (1 inch total on a sash curtain); *for wide, flat rods*, add 1 inch; for round rods, add rod diameter.

8 To finished length, add top allowance and lower hem allowance (see individual project for specific figures) plus a 1-inch ravel allowance to determine cut length.

9 Multiply cut length by number of widths to get total length in inches. Divide result by 36 to arrive at number of yards to buy. Add about 5 percent more (a minimum of 1 yard) for flaws.

DETERMINING YARDAGE FOR PATTERNED FABRIC

If you plan to use a fabric with a printed or woven design, you'll no doubt have to buy extra yardage since, with few exceptions, the repeats in the pattern must be matched when you make your window treatment.

The calculations are the same as those for unpatterned fabric up to the cut length figure. It's this measurement that needs to be adjusted to account for the pattern repeat on your fabric.

MUST PATTERNS MATCH? A tiny pattern repeat—a dot or small floral pattern, for example—may not need to be matched for gathered styles, such as rod-pocket curtains. But don't let the size of the repeat fool you. Even the smallest patterns can look mismatched after the fabric has been seamed.

To see if small repeats will need matching, unroll enough yardage while you're in the store so you can lay two sections of the fabric side by side, selvages aligned. Matching motifs in the pattern, arrange the fabric sections to make the pattern continue across the two widths. Now shift one of the sections slightly.

If you can't see any difference in the pattern, you can calculate total yardage according to the directions for unpatterned fabrics. But if the pattern shifts, base your calculations on the size of the pattern repeat (see below).

MEASURING THE VERTICAL REPEAT. To find the extra yardage needed for matching patterns, you must measure and record the height of the pattern repeat, called the vertical repeat. Measure from one spot on one motif to the same spot in the next identical motif above it. That distance is the vertical repeat.

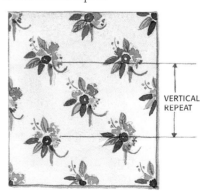

VERTICAL REPEAT

MATCHING WIDTHS. Most patterned fabric is designed so that horizontal repeats match at the selvages or just inside them.

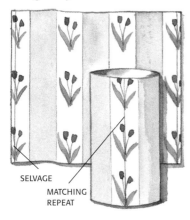

SELVAGE

MATCHING REPEAT

If the pattern matches farther into the width, you'll lose fabric when you stitch widths together. Check to see where patterned fabric matches before you buy it. If the distance from the inner edge of the selvage to the point where you'll stitch is more than an inch, don't buy the fabric.

PATTERN PLACEMENT. Repeats should match at seams on adjoining fabric widths, and the patterns should align horizontally on paired panels and on all window treatments in a room.

You have some flexibility in where the pattern repeats fall on the finished treatment. The usual approach is to place full repeats at the lower hem and allow the top of the treatment to end anywhere on the repeat. If you place the top of a full repeat at the top of the treatment, the pattern will be lost in the pleats or gathers.

When treatments are different at the top or bottom, place a full repeat at the bottom of the longest treatment. On the shorter treatment, place the pattern so the eye reads the repeats at the same level in all treatments.

REPEAT CUT LENGTH AND YARDAGE CALCULATIONS. You must adjust the cut length for your pattern repeat and recalculate to determine the total yardage:

1 Follow directions for steps 1–8 on pages 16–17.

2 Divide cut-length measurement by vertical repeat size. Round up to next whole number if result contains a fraction to arrive at number of pattern repeats needed for each cut length.

3 Multiply that number by vertical repeat to determine, in inches, the repeat cut length.

4 Multiply repeat cut length by number of fabric widths to get total length in inches. Divide by 36 inches to convert to yards.

THOSE FEW CRUCIAL INCHES. To make sure that pattern repeats will fall in the right place when your window treatment is made up, it's crucial to start measuring total yardage at the correct point in the pattern, rather than at the cut end of the yardage on the bolt. Usually, the cut end coming off the bolt is the bottom of the pattern, that is, the motifs run toward the center of the bolt. Study the pattern and look for arrows on the selvage to determine which way is up.

To have full repeats fall at the bottom of the treatment, unroll enough yardage to find the full repeat that would end at the lower fold. Measure below that for the hem allowance; begin to measure total yardage there.

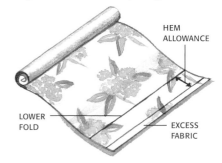

HEM ALLOWANCE

LOWER FOLD

EXCESS FABRIC

adding linings and interlinings

The benefits of lining window treatments far outweigh their added cost and construction time. A lining adds insulation, provides a greater degree of privacy, and protects the face fabric. It also improves the appearance of window treatments both on the inside and outside of your home.

Most lining fabrics are made of cotton or cotton/polyester or polyester/rayon blends. Sateen, a strong, tightly woven lining fabric, comes in white and a range of off-whites. For a uniform appearance from the outside, use the same color lining for all window treatments.

For energy efficiency and light control, use insulating (thermal) and blackout linings, which are laminated with vinyl or foam acrylic.

Cotton flannel is often used to interline a window treatment, adding body and insulating qualities as well as blocking noise and light. An interlining fabric is cut to the same size as the face fabric; they are basted together on all the edges before the window treatment construction begins. The face fabric and interlining are then used as one fabric.

before you sew

WHETHER YOU'RE SEWING a single shade or draping a wall of windows, you'll undoubtedly have to handle much more fabric than for most sewing projects. You'll need plenty of room and probably some special tools.

space to work

Staking out and organizing a special work area is worth the time it takes, even if it steals some living space for a while. A sewing room with a large table and special nooks and crannies for supplies is ideal. If you don't have the luxury of a sewing room and table, you'll need a large, flat surface on which to measure, cut, and sew.

As an alternative to a table, consider a piece of plywood or a hollow flush door. As a base for either one, you can use a pair of sawhorses or a table (protected with a blanket). If you choose sawhorses, you'll need rigid plywood 3/4 to 1 inch thick. It's best to pad your work surface. For details, see page 20.

tools of the trade

The following list includes all the tools necessary for making window treatments, as well as some that are very useful though not essential.

MEASURING TOOLS

A spring-return 12-foot or longer *steel tape measure* assures accurate measuring of windows. For measuring fabric, a 100-inch synthetic tape is convenient.

An *L-square*, available at art supply stores, is essential for squaring off the ends of yardage. A 12-by-24-inch L-square is better than a smaller one, and a lightweight artist's type is easier to handle than a heavy carpenter's model.

A 32-by-40-inch piece of *mat board* with the corners cut exactly square is an alternative to an L-square.

A metal or wood *straightedge* is useful for marking and extending

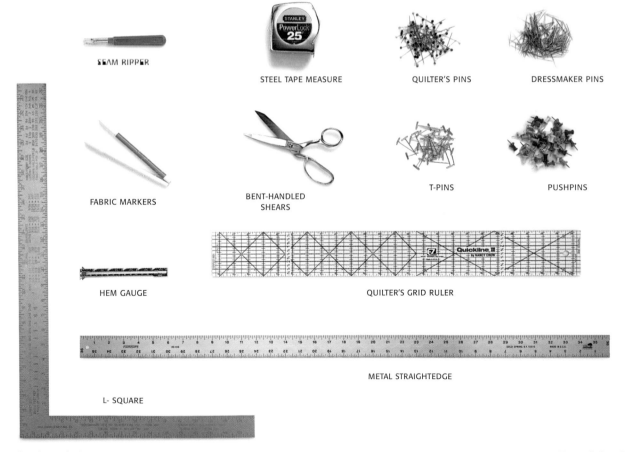

SEAM RIPPER

STEEL TAPE MEASURE

QUILTER'S PINS

DRESSMAKER PINS

FABRIC MARKERS

BENT-HANDLED SHEARS

T-PINS

PUSHPINS

HEM GAUGE

QUILTER'S GRID RULER

METAL STRAIGHTEDGE

L- SQUARE

Sewing window treatments is much easier when you have the right tools and supplies for each step of the process. Essential tools include measuring tools for accuracy, cutting tools that are sharp and appropriate for the material being cut, a steam iron and ironing accessories, a sewing machine in good working order, and sewing supplies.

cutting lines. Available in a variety of sizes, a clear *quilter's grid ruler* at least 18 inches long and 3 inches wide is especially helpful in marking hems.

Handy for measuring and marking fabric, a *cardboard cutting board* or a gridded cutting mat can also be used as a guide when pleating swags.

To mark cutting lines, hems, and pleats, you'll need a *fabric marker.* Your choices are many, from traditional chalk to pens and pencils. Choose a chalk marker that makes a fine, consistent line and does not have to be sharpened. Experiment on your fabric before choosing a marking pen. Some leave permanent marks.

A *hem gauge* is a 6-inch ruler with an adjustable slide that aids in measuring seam allowances and lower and side hems.

CUTTING TOOLS

Easier on the hands than scissors, *bent-handled shears* allow the fabric to lie flat while you cut. Choose an 8- or 9-inch-long pair for quick cutting. To make long, even cuts, you can choose longer *dressmaking shears.*

IRONING TOOLS

A *steam iron* is the most versatile ironing tool because it adjusts to suit a wide variety of fabrics. To steam out wrinkles and freshen up window coverings after they're hung, try a *hand steamer.*

Since you'll need a larger surface than an ironing board offers, consider padding a *large table* or piece of plywood instead, as described below.

Keep a *plastic spray bottle* handy near the ironing surface for extra

moisture. Always test a sample of your fabric first to avoid water spotting.

SEWING TOOLS

Your *sewing machine* needs to be in good working order. Clean it before every project; maintain it as indicated in the owner's manual. A serger is not essential, but it certainly saves time in finishing edges and makes your work look more professional.

A strip of *masking tape* laid down on the throat plate of your sewing machine serves as a handy guide for keeping seams and hems straight. For hints on using tape, see page 28.

Always use *sewing machine needles* that are compatible with the weight of your fabric. The heavier the fabric or the more it is layered, the higher the number on the needle. Use a 70/10 for sheer fabrics, an 80/12 for medium-weight fabrics, and a 90/14 or above for heavy fabrics and for tacking pleats.

A packet of *hand-sewing needles* in assorted sizes should take care of most hand-sewing jobs. But tacking pleats by hand will require an especially heavy-duty needle.

Fine, sharp *dressmaker pins* number 20, $1^1/_4$ inches long, are the best to use. Glass heads on the pins won't melt under the iron, but plastic ones may. And remember to always remove pins instead of sewing over them.

Stronger than dressmaker pins are *T-pins,* useful for holding plush or open-weave fabrics. T-pins come in size 20 and size 24 (large). *Pushpins* are useful for holding pleats on swags and temporarily securing shades, valances, and swags to mounting boards.

A fine, sharp *seam ripper* speeds the task of taking out any imperfect rows of stitching.

padding a work surface

Covering your work surface with padding prevents your fabric from slipping and sliding and allows you to anchor the fabric as you're working.

COVERING A TABLE. Drape enough cotton (not polyester) batting on the table so you have at least a $^1/_2$-inch thickness. Starting at one end, pull the corners tightly and fasten them underneath with safety pins. Repeat at the other end. Tape any dangling edges.

Cover the padding with an unpatterned cotton sheet, muslin, or canvas. Smooth and fasten as you did the batting. Spray the surface with water; as the fabric dries, it will shrink over the padding.

PADDING A PLYWOOD SHEET OR A DOOR. Begin by laying a cotton sheet, muslin, or canvas on the floor and layering cotton batting on the fabric to a thickness of $^1/_2$ inch. Center the plywood or door on top. Starting at the middle of one long side, fold the batting and fabric over the edge and secure every 2 inches using a staple gun. Repeat to staple the opposite side, pulling tautly. Do the same on the remaining sides.

Return to the starting point and continue pulling and stapling the batting and fabric in 12-inch segments on both sides of the center until you've worked to the corners. Miter the corners and staple. Dampen as described above.

selecting and preparing fabric

CRUCIAL to the success of a window treatment is the fabric from which it's made. But selecting a suitable fabric from the dizzying array available in fabric stores and sample books can be tiring and frustrating. That's why it's important to know what to look for in a fabric and how to prepare it so it will hang evenly and drape smoothly.

shopping tips

You'll find the best fabric selection, as well as the most knowledgeable salespeople, in stores that specialize in fabrics for home decorating. Other good sources include full-service fabric stores, which often have home decorating fabric sections, and interior decorators and designers, who have access to fabrics from many sources.

LOOKING AT FABRIC

Choosing fabric involves more than simply picking a color or pattern that you like. Here are some guidelines.

APPEARANCE. Undoubtedly, your first consideration as you browse among the bolts of fabric will be appearance. When you shop, take along paint chips and fabric swatches to compare colors, textures, and patterns with those of your walls and furnishings.

Because background color and lighting can alter a fabric's appearance, try to take an entire bolt of fabric home with you for a day or two. Or buy a yard of fabric and hang it at the window you're planning to cover. Check for ease of sewing, and whether it wrinkles easily or shows water spots.

When you are in the store, unroll several yards and gather one end in your hand. Does it drape well? Does it have the necessary weight for the treatment you're considering? Does

the design or texture hold its own, without getting lost in the folds?

Stand back several feet so you can see how the fabric looks from a distance.

GRAIN. To drape properly, fabric must have as straight a grain as possible, that is, its crosswise threads should run perpendicular to its lengthwise threads.

The selvage is parallel to the lengthwise grain. You will need to establish the crosswise grain. This can be accomplished by clipping into the selvage and tearing the fabric from selvage to selvage. If the fabric does not tear easily, then clip the fabric past the selvage and draw out a thread as far as possible until it breaks. Cut along the space that is created. Draw out another strand of thread and continue cutting.

Be very careful when selecting a patterned fabric. The less expensive the fabric, the more likely that the print will be slightly off-grain, veering at an angle from the crosswise threads. Usually, the misalignment isn't severe enough to be noticeable. But if you're not sure about the pattern, take a closer look.

To check patterned fabric, fold the fabric horizontally, wrong side in, aligning the selvages. If the print runs evenly along the fold, it's well aligned with the fabric grain. But if it wanders across the fold, the print is badly off-grain.

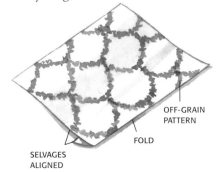

OFF-GRAIN PATTERN

FOLD

SELVAGES ALIGNED

Because it's virtually impossible to straighten the grain, don't buy any fabric on which the pattern is off by more than $1/2$ inch across the width.

FINISHES. Finishes added to fabrics prevent wrinkles and mildew and discourage insects. The most useful finishes, however, are those that repel stains and soil. Silicone finishes seal fibers, allowing you to wipe away water-based stains. Fluorochemical finishes repel both water and oil-based stains and last through several dry cleanings. Note that some finishes make the fabric more difficult to sew.

BUYING FABRIC

Once you've selected your fabric, buy all you need at one time (plus an extra $1/2$ yard for sample pressing and stitching). If possible, buy all the fabric from one bolt. If the amount of fabric left on a bolt is too little for your project, special-order a full bolt.

CHECKING DYE LOTS. Most fabrics are marked with a dye lot number on the store tag. If you're using fabric from two different dye lots, hold the fabrics together and examine them in different light; look for any perceptible differences in the colors. If you can't see any, you're probably safe.

But to ensure the best results, don't mix fabric from different bolts at the same window. For example, if you have three windows, buy enough from one bolt to make treatments for two of them; then, from another bolt, buy all of the fabric for the third window. To do this, you'll need to think in terms of cut lengths instead of total yardage when the fabric is being measured. Mark the pieces so you won't mix them up while you're sewing.

a *fabric collection*

Fabric, whether made from a natural fiber or a synthetic, is the key to a beautiful window covering. Good fabric drapes well, pleats crisply, and has more body—all characteristics of a professional-looking window treatment.

SHEER
Sheer fabrics, with their open weaves and delicate yarns, filter light and offer limited privacy. Cotton, linen, and polyester are fibers commonly used in sheer fabrics.

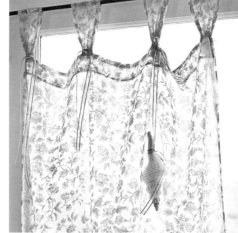 

MEDIUM-WEIGHT
Medium-weight fabrics are favorites with home sewers because they are easy to handle. From plain linen weaves to bold chintzes, from striped sheeting to convenient blends, medium-weight fabrics are the most versatile choice for many styles.

HEAVY-WEIGHT
Sumptuous satins and silks and full-bodied cottons and rayon velvets make elegant window dressings that can be used in a variety of rooms from casual to formal.

mixing and matching

The best-dressed windows often feature several fabrics in a combination of patterns or textures. You can use plaids and stripes, florals and checks, in coordinating or contrasting colors. Often a simple contrast border in a solid color plain or textured fabric will provide just enough accent to enhance a design without overwhelming it. Bows, buttons, tassels, fringe, and rosettes are the jewelry that accessorizes the final look.

INSPECTING FABRIC FOR FLAWS.
If you're buying fabric off a bolt, hold it up to the light and inspect it for small holes or inconsistencies in the weave. Sometimes, flaws are marked along the selvage with tape or pins. Ask to have extra fabric to allow for the flaws or choose not to purchase the fabric. Always buy 5 percent more fabric (a minimum of 1 yard) to account for any flaws.

PRESHRINKING AND CLEANING YOUR FABRIC. It is generally not a good idea to preshrink home decorating fabric. Preshrinking can wash away the fabric's protective finish and cause it to lose its fresh, crisp appearance.

As a rule, it's a good idea to dry-clean treatments made from home decorating fabrics. Unlined curtains are about the only treatment that may be successfully laundered.

CHOOSING THREAD

All-purpose 100 percent cotton thread works well for all fabrics and blends. Polyester thread is sometimes used for synthetic fabrics, but it stretches slightly when sewn and has a tendency to pucker.

When matching thread to fabric, choose thread that's a slightly darker shade than the fabric. For prints, match the thread to the background or the most predominant color. Use the same thread color for serging and finishing edges.

how to cut lengths

To cut your fabric into the lengths required for your project, you'll need the cut length or repeat cut length measurement from your window treatment work sheet (see page 16);

a large, flat work surface; an L-square; a straightedge; and chalk or a fabric marker. Use one of the following methods, depending on whether your fabric is unpatterned or patterned.

UNPATTERNED FABRIC

For fabric with no discernible pattern, you'll need to square off one cut end of the yardage; then you can begin cutting lengths.

SQUARING OFF THE FABRIC. To begin, lay the fabric, right side up, on a flat surface.

A good way to create a cutting guide is to pull a crosswise thread, if possible. Cut into the fabric beyond the selvage near one cut end. Pick up one thread and pull it across the width. If the thread breaks, cut farther into the fabric next to the thread and pick it up again.

If you can't pull a thread, align the short blade of the L-square along one selvage of the fabric, close to one cut end, at the point where you'll be able to mark a line across the full width of the fabric. Using the other blade of the square as a straightedge, draw a line perpendicular to the selvage.

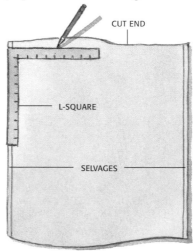

Remove the L-square and use a straightedge to extend the line 12 inches at a time to the opposite selvage. With the square, check that the line meets the opposite selvage at a true right angle. Cut along the line.

CUTTING LENGTHS. Measure down each selvage a distance equal to the cut length; clip selvages at this point. Using a straightedge, draw a line across the fabric between the clips. With an L-square, check each corner for squareness.

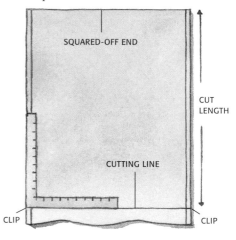

Cut along the line; this is the first squared-off length.

Continue to measure, mark, and cut until all lengths are cut. To avoid sewing one width to another upside down, make a small notch in the selvage at the lower right corner of each length.

PATTERNED FABRIC

Some prints and woven pattern repeats run slightly off-grain. When you cut these fabrics for window treatments, follow the lines of the pattern rather than the grain of the fabric.

Once all the widths have been seamed, you can then square off the bottom edge.

planning arched panels

BEFORE CUTTING PANELS with a curved upper edge, make a pattern to ensure that the curve will be correct once you've added fullness—an incorrect curve will cause the panels to hang off-grain. Begin by making a template of the window shape; do not include any fullness.

1 Use tape or pushpins to fix paper over the curved portion of the window, and trace the outline. Remove the template, fold it in half vertically, and make sure the two halves are identical; square off the lower edge.

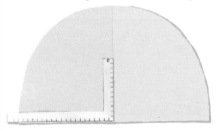

Cut the template in half vertically and discard one half.

2 Decide the fullness of the finished panel (page 17, step 3). On a larger piece of paper, draft a rectangle this width by the depth of the template.

3 Using an L-square and pencil, draw several lines perpendicular to the bottom edge on the template. The lines should intersect the curved upper edge at regular intervals. Cut the template apart on the vertical lines.

4 Position the cut-apart template on the large drafted rectangle, aligning the outer vertical edges and the straight bottom edge, and spreading the pieces evenly across the rectangle. If part of the curve is steep, split the pieces in that area again. Tape down the pieces. On the rectangle, draw a new curve that skims the curve of the cut-apart pieces.

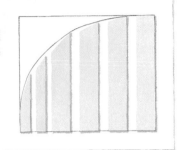

5 Make sure your pattern height incorporates the desired coverage above the window (page 14); note on the pattern the length below the curved area. Cut out the pattern. When ready to sew, join the widths and sew the hems (pages 26-28), and then cut the top shape using your pattern—be sure to reverse the pattern for opposite panels. Use a bias strip to face the top edge and make the rod pocket if required.

These arched draperies have been gathered and fixed to a board; they are trimmed with cord, Maltese crosses, and a pair of tassels. Invisible rigging holds them open.

SQUARING OFF FIRST END. On a flat surface, lay out several yards of fabric, wrong side up. At the cut end, bring the selvages together in the center, forming a tube. Look to see where the motifs—a flower, a leaf, a geometric shape—match.

Mark the matching points on each selvage where you started measuring total yardage when you bought the fabric. Unfold the fabric, turn it right side up, and, using a straightedge, connect the marks to make your cutting line. Cut along this line.

CUTTING LENGTHS. To cut the first length, follow the instructions for unpatterned fabric (see page 24), substituting your repeat cut-length figure for the cut length.

To cut additional lengths, tape the uncut fabric down, right side up. Lay the first cut length, right side up, on top, carefully positioning it so the motifs in the pattern repeats match perfectly.

Mark the cutting point on each selvage; remove the top piece and use a straightedge to mark the cutting line. Then cut along the marked line. Repeat for each successive length.

To avoid confusion when you sew widths together, mark pieces by making a small notch in the selvage at the lower right corner of each length.

SQUARING OFF JOINED WIDTHS. If, after joining widths, the top and bottom edges aren't square, you'll need to square and trim the bottom. The top edge will be squared when you measure and mark the hem, the finished length, and the top allowance.

With the panel right side up, lay a carpenter's square along the selvage on the short edge. Mark a line perpendicular to the selvage; extend the line 12 inches at a time to keep it straight. You'll have a triangular segment left at the bottom.

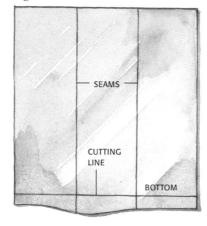

Before you cut on the marked line, be sure you will have enough fabric at the top. With some patterned fabrics, the repeat cut length will provide the extra fabric you'll need to square the bottom and still give you the required inches at the top.

Measure the hem allowance plus the finished length from the marked line. From this point, measure the top allowance and check to be sure that it doesn't go beyond the shorter edge. If it does extend beyond, you'll need to decrease slightly the depth of your hem and/or heading.

TRIMMING SELVAGES. Some selvages are woven tighter than the fabric and tend to draw up. If your fabric is unpatterned, trim the selvages before joining widths. With some patterned fabrics, the pattern matches so close to the selvages that seam allowances will be reduced if you trim the selvages first. If the selvages and fabric lie flat, you do not need to trim the selvages.

JOINING AND TRIMMING FABRIC WIDTHS. For a neat appearance, full widths of fabric should hang at the leading edge of a treatment. Place partial widths on the sides. For draperies, a partial width must be at least half a width. On a single panel treatment, center a full width.

For an unpatterned fabric, join widths with ½-inch seams. For a perfect match on patterned fabric, lay widths right sides together with selvages aligned. Fold back the selvage edges until the pattern matches exactly. Press the fold lightly.

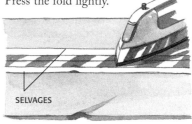

Unfold the selvage edges, pin the layers, and stitch on the fold.

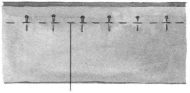

STITCH ALONG FOLD

After seaming widths, trim the panel to the total width required.

sewing simplified

SEWING window treatments is about as simple as sewing can be. Here are a few basic techniques that will help speed the work.

hand-sewing techniques

Hand sewing is used for temporary stitching or for finishing. Use a single, rather than double, strand of thread and wax it for better control. For temporary stitching, do not knot the thread; secure it with a couple of small stitches instead.

If you are left-handed, reverse the terms *right* and *left* in the following directions.

SLIPSTITCH. The slipstitch provides an almost invisible finish for hems, linings, and trims. Working from right to left, insert the needle into the folded edge of the upper layer, slide it inside the fold, bring it out 1/8 to 1/4 inch from the insertion point, and then slide the needle under a single thread of the lower layer. Repeat. When slipstitching braids or other trims, slide the needle through and along the woven or twisted edge, concealing the thread.

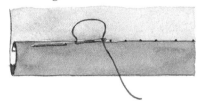

BLINDSTITCH. The blindstitch is used for hemming and holding facings in place, and is inconspicuous on both sides. First, finish the cut edge of the hem or facing. Roll this edge back about 1/4 inch. Working from right to left, make a small horizontal stitch

under one thread of the fabric, then under a thread of the hem or facing diagonally opposite the first stitch.

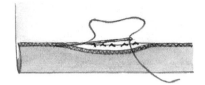

CATCHSTITCH. The catchstitch holds two overlapping layers of fabric in place while allowing some flexibility in their alignment. Use it to attach the edges of hems and facings to the wrong side of fabrics. Work from left to right, but insert the needle from right to left. Make a small horizontal stitch in one layer, then make a second stitch diagonally opposite the first in the other layer. Repeat, alternating stitches along the edge in a zigzag fashion and keeping the threads loose.

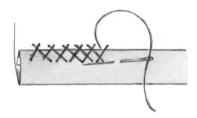

machine-sewing techniques

The directions in this book call for a variety of machine stitches including finishing edges and seams, hems, and topstitching. All are explained below.

SERGED EDGE OR SEAM. A serger produces an overlocking stitch to prevent raveling and, at the same time, trims excess fabric from the seam allowance. A three-thread stitch is commonly used as an edge finish. A four-thread stitch can sew the seam and finish the edge in one pass.

ZIGZAG EDGE AND SEAM. A zigzag stitch sewn along the raw edge of a fabric allows it to lie flat and prevents raveling. Center presser foot over raw edge of your fabric and zigzag-stitch, allowing needle to stitch both on and off fabric an even distance.

A zigzag seam is a sturdy, ravel-proof seam. Place the fabric right sides together. Stitch on the seamline, using a narrow, short zigzag, 1mm wide and 1mm long. In the seam allowance, stitch another zigzag, 2mm wide and 2mm long. Trim the excess seam allowance. This seam is especially useful on loosely woven and stretchy fabrics.

DOUBLE HEM. Both side and lower hems are doubled to make the fabric hang better. For most projects, the lower hem goes in before the side hems.

To make a double hem, turn up the lower edge of the hem allowance, wrong sides together, and press. Turn the raw edge in to meet the pressed fold and press again. Hem by hand or machine close to the second fold.

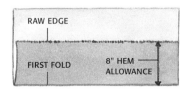

RAW EDGE

FIRST FOLD

8" HEM ALLOWANCE

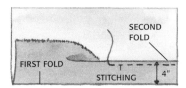

SECOND FOLD

FIRST FOLD

STITCHING

4"

Repeat for the lining, adjusting the first fold to the total hem allowance.

Make a double side hem in the same way, using the total side hem allowances as the guide for the first fold. Hand-stitch the opening closed at the lower edge.

If a fabric has a loose weave or is particularly heavy, it may stretch after hanging. Instead of stitching the hem, baste it and hang the treatment for a week or so. Then adjust the hem and stitch.

MITER ADJOINING HEMS. With this method, you can miter adjoining hems whether symmetrical or asymmetrical.

Mark and press adjacent hems in place. Mark intersection where hem edges meet, placing a pin in the fold of each hem. Mark lower corner with pin.

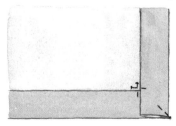

Open out the folds, keeping the pins in place. Turn hem, right sides together, keeping the first fold turned under and matching the pins. Mark a diagonal line from the pins on folded edges to the corner pin. (Fabric edges will line up for a symmetrical miter

but not for an asymmetrical miter.) Stitch along marked line.

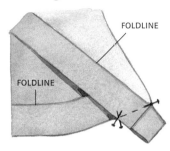

FOLDLINE

FOLDLINE

Before trimming the seam, turn the corner right side out to be sure it's correct. Then turn back and trim seam allowance to $1/4$ inch. Finger-press seam allowance open, turn right side out, and press again. Topstitch hems in place.

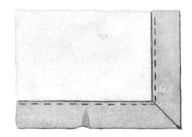

a tape trick

Masking tape can help keep seams and hems straight and parallel.

For a seam guide, measure to the right of the needle a distance equal to the seam allowance. On the machine, place a strip of tape with the left edge at this point, parallel to the stitching line. As you sew, keep the seam allowance aligned with the tape's edge.

For a hem guide, measure $1/8$ inch less than hem width; tape. The stitches will run just inside the inner fold of the hem.

WEIGHTS. Weights sewn into the lower corners of each panel and at each seam make full-length panels hang straighter. Either purchase covered weights or enclose weights in small pockets of fabric.

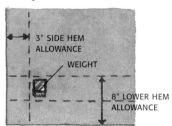

3" SIDE HEM ALLOWANCE

WEIGHT

8" LOWER HEM ALLOWANCE

BLINDHEM. Most sewing machines come with a blindhem presser foot that makes a perfect hidden stitch. After pressing the hem to the wrong side, fold the project body away from the hem, exposing about $1/4$ inch of the wrong side of the hem edge. Align the presser foot guide blade along the fold of the project body; set the machine to a blindhem stitch. The needle will sew about five stitches on the hem only and then cross over with a zigzag stitch to catch the project body. Check your machine guide book for exact settings.

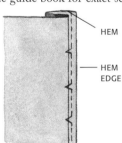

HEM

HEM EDGE

TOPSTITCH. Topstitching can be decorative, functional, or both. Using a regular stitch length, stitch through one or more layers of fabric with the face fabric right side up in the machine. To ensure accuracy, baste from the wrong side first and topstitch on the right side using the basting as a guide.

Marking the line with chalk on the right side also helps in stitching a straight line.

GATHERS. For ease of handling, use gathers to control the fullness in a length of fabric that will be sewn to another piece, as when making a ruffle. Gathers can be adjustable, so you can manipulate and distribute the fullness as desired. If you have a ruffler foot or attachment, the gathers can be stitched to a set tension; these will be even but cannot be tightened or loosened, so refer to the attachment manual and make a test piece.

For basted adjustable gathers, make two parallel rows of basting stitches, one on the seamline, one just inside the seam allowance. Pull the bobbin threads to gather the fabric to the desired fullness; wrap them in a figure eight around a pin to secure temporarily.

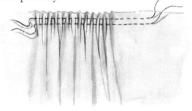

For zigzag adjustable gathers, lay button thread or crochet cotton over the seamline and zigzag stitch over it. Pull the button thread to gather the fabric to the desired fullness; wrap it in a figure eight around a pin to secure temporarily.

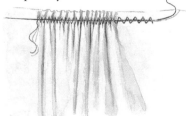

CUTTING BIAS STRIPS. To find the bias, place one leg of a 45-degree right-angle triangle on the selvage and mark along the hypotenuse, or fold the fabric diagonally so the crosswise threads are parallel to the selvage and mark the fold. You can mark and cut the strips individually, but here is an efficient way to cut large quantities.

Mark the longest possible bias line on your fabric and cut along it. Beginning at one 45-degree corner, fold the fabric repeatedly, aligning the bias edge. Mark strips of the desired width parallel to the bias edge and cut through all layers—pin first to keep the layers aligned.

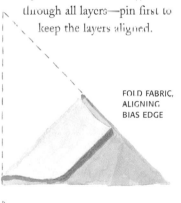

FOLD FABRIC, ALIGNING BIAS EDGE

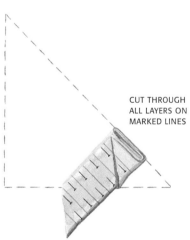

CUT THROUGH ALL LAYERS ON MARKED LINES

JOINING BIAS STRIPS. Press-stretch bias strips before working with them for easier handling and smoother results. Before joining the strips, check to see that their ends are on the straight

grain; recut if necessary. Place two strips right sides together, with the ends aligned as shown, and sew together.

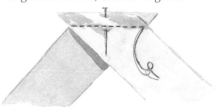

WELTING/PIPING. To make welting/piping, put a zipper or piping foot on your machine, aligning it to the left of the needle. Center cable cord on the wrong side of a bias strip. Fold the strip over the cord, aligning cut edges—there is no need to pin. Feed the cord and bias into the machine with the cord to the right of the needle and the seam allowance to the left, under the foot. Stitch close to the cord, continuing to fold the bias over the cord as you sew.

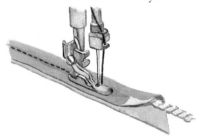

To attach welting/piping, pin it to the right side of the project piece, aligning the cut edges. Position the zipper or piping foot to the right of your needle, and feed the piece into the machine, welting side up, with the cord to the left of the needle and the seam allowance to the right, under the foot.

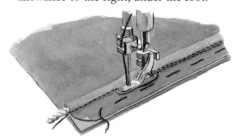

window treatment projects

THE BEAUTIFUL FABRICS and wealth of hardware styles available make it easier than ever for anyone with basic sewing skills to create customized window treatments. It's not only practical to sew your own window fashions, it's fun, too. Plus the result will be exactly what you desire, enhancing your decor and reflecting your personal style.

On the following pages you'll find inspiring photos and instructions for a variety of window treatments, from easy-to-make curtains to more complicated swags and cascades. Choose whichever style suits your taste and needs, read the directions, purchase your materials, and get started.

curtains

RIGHT: *Sheer curtains have large grommets in the top hem that are threaded over the rod. The look is modern and tailored.*

BELOW: *Outside-mounted rod pocket café curtains, topped with a companion valance, lend a classic finish to a pretty bathroom. Add a roller shade or blind for privacy.*

OPPOSITE, CLOCKWISE FROM TOP LEFT:
*Muslin rod pocket curtains on flat rods
add an airy finish to a window wall;
these puddle slightly. On a pair of
windows, two single panels, with
holdbacks on opposite sides, create a
formal effect—even when the panels are
informal tab curtains. The turned-down
lining forms a small cuff at the top of
these plain curtains. Swept-back
curtains provide privacy with panache
on the arched entry to this bathing nook,
where a matching Roman shade dresses
the window beyond.*

ABOVE: *Curtains with a deep, stiffened
top hem fall in crisp regular folds
when opened. These are hooked onto a
hidden traverse rod and look a lot like
draperies, but they're much easier to
make because they're not pleated—you
could get a similar effect hanging them
from rings.*

RIGHT: *Colorful dishtowels with ribbon
tabs hung as tiered curtains prove that
great style can be quick and easy—you
can make these in just a few minutes,
even if you've never sewn before.*

ABOVE: *Eyelets in the top hem of these blanket-patterned panels enable them to be laced onto a rustic pole. For a dressier look, try this with velvet panels and gold cord.*

RIGHT: *A small tablecloth draped over these rod pocket curtains adds a sweet complement to the ruffled effect of the curtain heading.*

FAR RIGHT: *This trio of white tie-tab curtains makes a simple frame for a garden view. Their top edge drapes informally when the tabs are pushed together.*

how to make curtains

TODAY'S CURTAINS offer myriad style possibilities, from elegant full-length panels to simple sash or tailored tab versions. The projects explained here reflect the diversity of curtain styles. Best of all, you'll discover that curtains are easy—and fun—to make.

a look at hardware

Choose curtain hardware in a style to complement the fabric you're using as well as the design of the curtains and rooms where they'll hang. Look for hardware in discount and department stores, home improvement centers, and large fabric stores that specialize in home decorating fabrics. Most curtain hardware from these retail sources is manufactured by just a few companies. For something more unusual, shop through mail-order sources, consult an interior decorator, or look for shops specializing in decorative hardware.

RODS AND POLES

Most metal rods are adjustable; most wood poles are not. Generally, rods and poles rest in brackets attached to the wall or window frame.

Rounded *café rods*, available in a range of sizes, styles, and finishes, are designated for café or full-length curtains that are gathered on the rod or hung on rings.

Flat curtain rods, either single or double, hold lightweight rod-pocket curtains or valances. If you're using a sheer fabric for rod-pocket curtains, look for clear rods that won't show through the fabric. Flexible clear rods are used for sunburst curtains.

For corner or bay windows, choose adjustable hinged flat or decorative rods, also called swing rods or portiere rods.

Wide flat rods, available in 2¹/₂- and 4¹/₂-inch widths, require an extra-wide rod pocket, adding visual depth and interest to traditional curtain styles.

Sash rods attach with shallow brackets to the top and bottom of the window frame. They are used on French doors and casement windows to hold sash or hourglass curtains.

Oval or round *tension rods* have a spring-tension mechanism to hold the plastic- or rubber-tipped rod within the window frame. Often, they're the only practical choice for recessed windows. Support a width greater than 36 inches with cup hooks.

Wood poles, used with decorative brackets and finials, lend distinction to rod-pocket or tab curtains. With the addition of matching wood rings, poles are also suitable for flat curtain panels.

Sleek, contemporary *cable rods* consist of a twisted wire cable that is cut to measure, streamlined rings, and end support brackets. This system's minimalist look works well in simple contemporary applications.

ACCESSORIES

Many of the following accessories can be found where curtain hardware is sold or in the notions section of stores that carry home decorating fabrics.

Finials are decorative pieces that attach to the ends of poles that aren't mitered or finished with elbows.

Unobtrusive *wood sockets* support poles for inside-mounted curtains; they are screwed to the window frame.

To increase the length by which the rod returns to the wall, attach *extension plates* to ordinary brackets.

Rings for curtains have small clips or eyelets on the bottom, which attach to the top edge of a curtain; they must be removed before the curtain is dry-cleaned. If the eyelets are large, you can use them in combination with 1-inch drapery hooks; pin the hooks to the back of the curtain heading and slip through the eyelets.

Valance hooks, designed for stationary treatments, fit over rods.

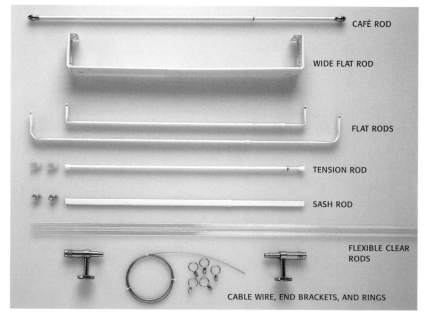

CAFÉ ROD

WIDE FLAT ROD

FLAT RODS

TENSION ROD

SASH ROD

FLEXIBLE CLEAR RODS

CABLE WIRE, END BRACKETS, AND RINGS

These curtain rods hold sheer and lightweight treatments. The cable rod system can support a light- to medium-weight curtain but is limited in the length it can span.

Jumbo grommets provide an opening that can be threaded over a rod. Use them instead of rod pockets or rings.

hardware installation

Mount your hardware *after* you've finished your project. Be sure to follow the manufacturer's instructions.

Where you install the hardware depends how you planned your curtain. You'll need to refer to your window treatment work sheet (page 16), to find the side extensions; mark those points at the window opening.

If your curtain has no heading, the top of the rod goes at the distance above the window opening noted on your work sheet. For a curtain with a heading, subtract the heading size from the distance the treatment extends above the opening. For example, if you planned to cover 5 inches above the window opening and your heading measures 2 inches, the top of the rod goes 3 inches above the opening.

To determine where to position the brackets, place the rod in a bracket and measure the distance from the top of the rod to the top screw hole in the bracket; add this distance to the previous figure and mark this point at the top of the window opening.

Install one bracket, attaching the top screw at the point you just marked. Place one end of the rod in the bracket and have a helper hold up the other end in its bracket. Before attaching the second bracket, check the rod with a carpenter's level. When the rod is level, mark the top screw hole for the second bracket and screw it to the wall.

If you're not able to screw into the studs, use expansion bolts, also called molly bolts. Plastic anchors are good for lightweight treatments or when you're installing concealed tieback holders.

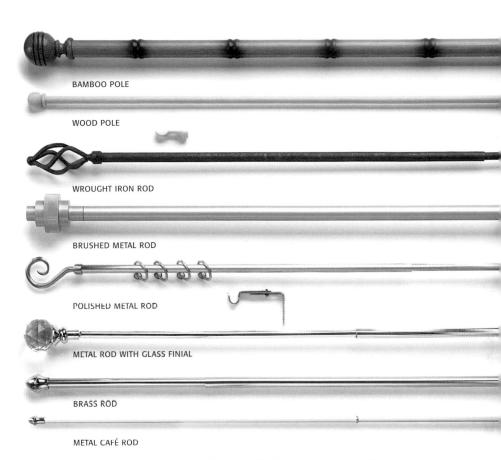

BAMBOO POLE

WOOD POLE

WROUGHT IRON ROD

BRUSHED METAL ROD

POLISHED METAL ROD

METAL ROD WITH GLASS FINIAL

BRASS ROD

METAL CAFÉ ROD

Decorative wood and metal curtain rods are available with a variety of finial styles and may come with coordinating rings and small brackets.

covering a finial with fabric

1 Cut a fabric square about 3 inches longer on each side than the circumference of the finial ball.

2 Install the finials.

3 Center the wrong side of the fabric square against the end of the finial. Smooth the fabric over the finial, gathering it at the base. Secure tightly with a rubber band, a piece of elastic, or sturdy string. Arrange the fabric evenly around the finial.

4 Trim the fabric so that it extends about 1 inch over the panel pocket; notch the extending fabric as needed to reduce bulk.

5 Tuck the extending fabric neatly inside the fabric rod pocket to conceal it.

flat panels

SIMPLE AND SPEEDY to sew, this basic curtain style can be attached to a rod with rings or tabs, and the panel can be lined or unlined. This project is good for beginners—calculations and stitching are easy as can be.

CALCULATING YARDAGE

Measure your window and fill in the window treatment work sheet (see pages 14–18). Flat panels do not have returns. For fullness, allow only 1½ to 2 times the finished width, rather than the usual 2½. Use the following allowances in your calculations:

LOWER HEM	8"
SIDE HEMS	6" TOTAL
TOP HEM	3"

UNLINED FLAT PANELS STEP-BY-STEP

1 Choose and prepare fabric, and join the fabric widths (see pages 21–26). Press seams open.

2 Fold and stitch lower hems (see page 27).

3 Fold and stitch side hems (see page 28).

4 On right side of fabric, measure from lower edge a distance equal to finished length. Mark with pins every 4 inches across panel.

5 Measure and mark 3-inch top hem allowance above pin-marked finished-length line. Trim ravel allowance.

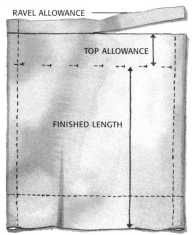

6 Fold down top edge, wrong side in, along finished-length line; press. Remove pins. Turn raw edge in to meet pressed fold and press again. Stitch close to second fold.

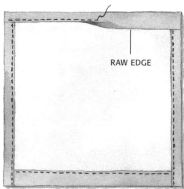

LINED FLAT PANELS STEP-BY-STEP

Use the following allowances when calculating yardage:

	FABRIC	LINING
LOWER HEM	8"	4"
SIDE HEMS	3" TOTAL	2½" TOTAL
TOP SEAM	1½"	NONE

1 Follow steps 1, 2, and 4, "Unlined flat panels," this page, for face fabric; follow steps 1 and 2 for lining. (Do not stitch side seams.)

2 Place lining on face fabric, right sides together, so lower edge of lining is 1 inch above lower edge of face fabric. Starting at leading edge, align first seams of face fabric and lining.

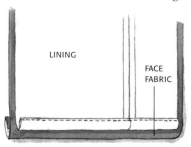

3 Trim face fabric or lining as needed so lining is ¼ inch narrower than face fabric at each side.

4 Trim lining so upper edge meets pin-marked finished-length line on face fabric. Then, on face fabric, measure and mark 1½ inches above finished-length line. Trim ravel allowance.

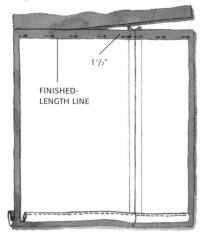

5 Remove lining. To face upper edge of lining so it doesn't show from front, cut a 4½-inch strip of face fabric equal in length to cut width of lining. With right sides together and raw edges aligned, pin and stitch the facing to the top edge of lining, using 1½-inch seam allowance. Press the facing up (it is a continuation of the lining).

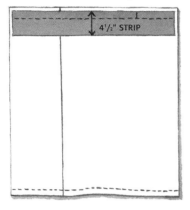

4½" STRIP

6 Place lining on face fabric, right sides together, with lower edge of lining 1 inch above lower edge of face fabric and side edges aligned (lining is slightly narrower); pin along sides. Sew together along sides and top, using 1½-inch seam allowance.

7 Turn panel right side out, lining side up, so an equal amount of face fabric shows at each side. Turning seam allowances toward center, press.

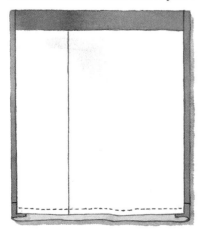

curtains on rings

Rings are a simple way to hang a curtain panel without gathering or pleating. To determine how many rings you'll need, divide width of each panel by 5 inches (a trial space size) to find approximate number of spaces between rings there will be; round off to nearest whole number for the actual number of spaces. Add 1 to this number to determine number of rings or hooks needed. Divide width by number of spaces for actual space size.

If you want the curtain to droop noticeably between rings, allow a larger space and use fewer rings or hooks; very tall or heavy panels may look better with a larger space too.

At each end of panel, sew or clip a ring to top edge; or insert point of drapery hook just below lower row of stitching. Space additional rings or hooks according to your calculations.

grommet heading

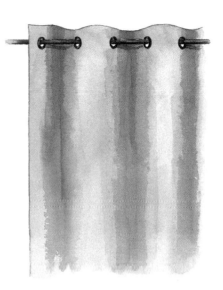

Grommets are an alternative to rings and work well for curtains that are not pulled back often. Using a tool provided by the manufacturer, install the grommets at equal intervals but no more than 8 inches apart; position the end ones 1½ inches in from the finished side edges.

To attach the curtain, you can thread the rod through the grommets as shown above. Or you can thread a decorative cord, a heavyweight ribbon, or a rope alternately through the grommets and over the rod, securing the cord to the rod or curtain at each end.

Be sure to plan for how you'll hang this kind of curtain before cutting (or at least before hemming) because it will determine where the top edge sits in relation to the rod and thus the total length.

adding decorative edgings

CUSTOM FINISHES, such as ruffles and banding, lend sophistication and style to ordinary window treatments. Ruffles usually decorate rod-pocket curtains; fabric bands can be added to flat panels or rod-pocket curtains.

ruffles

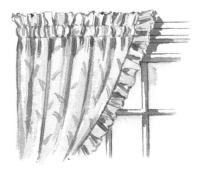

Ruffles can add texture and interest along the bottom of a shaped valance or down a curtain's leading edge.

MEASURING AND CALCULATING YARDAGE

Cutting ruffle strips on the crosswise grain is the most economical use of the fabric. Some patterns call for lengthwise strips. When you're working with a plaid or stripe fabric, consider bias-cut ruffles.

1 Taking into account the scale of treatment and fabric, determine finished width of ruffle (most are $1^{1}/_{2}$ to 3 inches wide). For a single-thickness hemmed ruffle, add 1 inch ($^{1}/_{2}$ inch for seam allowance and $^{1}/_{2}$ inch for a narrow hem) to finished width to arrive at cut width. For a folded ruffle (used more often), double the finished width and add 1 inch for two $^{1}/_{2}$-inch seam allowances.

2 Measure edges for ruffle and then multiply by 2 or $2^{1}/_{2}$ for total strip length. Divide total strip length by usable fabric width and round up to nearest whole number to determine the number of crosswise strips needed.

3 Multiply cut width of each strip by number of strips and divide result by 36 inches for yards needed.

MAKING RUFFLES

You'll need to sew together fabric strips to make ruffles.

1 Cut strips as needed. To join, arrange strips, right sides together, at a right angle and seam on bias. Trim seam allowance; press open.

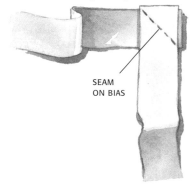

SEAM
ON BIAS

2 *For a hemmed ruffle*, fold each short edge in $^{1}/_{2}$ inch, wrong side in, and press; turn raw edge in to meet pressed fold and press again. Machine-stitch ends. Repeat along one long edge.

For a folded ruffle, fold pieced strip in half lengthwise, right side in, and stitch across ends, making $^{1}/_{4}$-inch seams. Turn right side out and press in half lengthwise.

3 Zigzag over a cord (buttonhole twist) about $^{3}/_{8}$ inch from raw edge. Backstitch over cord at one end. When instructed to gather ruffle, pull cord.

ATTACHING RUFFLES

To attach a single-thickness ruffle or a folded ruffle to the side edges of an unlined curtain, first remove the side hem allowances from the curtain, leaving $^{1}/_{2}$-inch seam allowances on each side. After making lower hem, serge the ruffle and panel together.

To attach a single-thickness ruffle or a folded ruffle to a lined curtain, trim the face fabric side hem allowances even with edge of lining.

1 Follow steps 1–2 and 4–5, "Unlined rod-pocket curtains," page 53, to make lower hems, measure and mark finished-length line, and trim top edge of face fabric and lining.

2 Divide ruffle strip and edge to be ruffled each into fourths, marking off each section with a pin. (Note that ruffle extends from the finished lower edge to the finished-length line at the top.)

3 With raw edges on right sides aligned, match pins on ruffle and curtain edge; pin. Gather ruffle strip to fit edge. Baste just inside zigzag line.

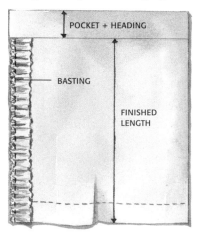

POCKET + HEADING

BASTING

FINISHED
LENGTH

4 Pin lining to face fabric, right sides together, sandwiching ruffle between layers. Sew together using 1/2-inch seam allowance. Remove gathering cord. Serge the seams together. Turn panel right sides out and press edges.

5 Press face fabric seam allowance on each side of pocket/heading allowance.

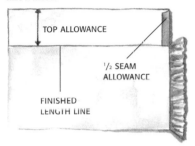

TOP ALLOWANCE

1/2 SEAM ALLOWANCE

FINISHED LENGTH LINE

6 Fold pocket/heading on finished-length line and press. Turn raw edge in to meet pressed fold and press again. Stitch pocket and heading, if used, as instructed in step 6, "Unlined rod-pocket curtains," page 53; stop stitching at the ruffle.

contrast banding

On both curtains and draperies, bands of fabric along the leading edges create a visual border. For lined panels you have two options: on-the-edge banding or set-in banding; this banding is attached after the lower hems are stitched but before the lining goes in.

For unlined panels, on-the-edge binding finishes the edges with clean miters at the corners. The side and lower hem allowances are removed to allow for these contrasting extensions.

ON-THE-EDGE BANDING

This simple trimming goes along the leading edge and wraps around to the wrong side.

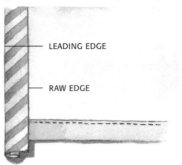

1 Cut a contrast strip two times desired finished width as seen from front plus 3 1/2 inches. Cut length of band is equal to distance from top cut edge of face fabric to 2 inches beyond lower hem fold.

2 Press and stitch lower hems on face fabric and lining. With right sides together and raw edges aligned at top and sides, stitch band to edge of face fabric, using seam allowance equal to width of finished band. Stitch to end of band.

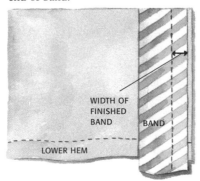

WIDTH OF FINISHED BAND

BAND

LOWER HEM

3 Turn panel wrong side up, with band extending, and press seam allowances toward band. Fold band against and over raw edges and press.

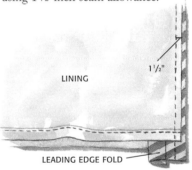

LEADING EDGE

RAW EDGE

4 Flip panel right side up and open up band. Pin lining to band, right sides together and raw edges aligned, positioning lower edge of lining 1 inch above lower edge of face fabric. Stitch using 1 1/2-inch seam allowance.

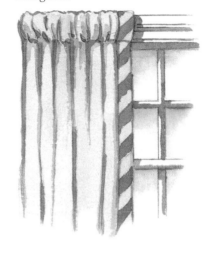

LINING

1 1/2"

LEADING EDGE FOLD

5 Press seam allowance toward band. (On back of panel, 1 1/2 inches of band will show.)

6 At lower edge, open lining, turn up band even with lower hem, and hand-stitch to hem.

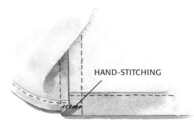

HAND-STITCHING

adding decorative edgings

ON-THE-EDGE BANDING WITH
MITERED CORNER: This banding
trims the leading edge and the hem
of the panel.

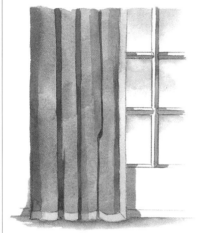

1 Determine finished width of
border. For the panel, subtract
lower hem and side hem allowances
plus finished band width, and then
add ¹/₂-inch seam allowances for cut
panel size.

   Cut a contrast strip twice the width
of finished binding, plus 1 inch for 2
seam allowances. Cut length of band
long enough to border curtain leading
edge plus lower edge plus several
inches (join several lengths as needed).

2 Press band in half lengthwise,
wrong side in. Press seam
allowances to the wrong side on both
long edges. Open out one folded seam
allowance and pin to edge of curtain,
right sides together. Starting at top of
one side, stitch along pressed foldline,
stopping just before corner at point
where seamlines intersect; backtack.

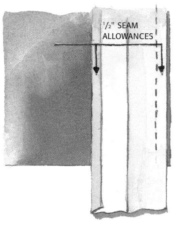

3 Keep outer seam allowance folded;
fold binding diagonally, wrong side
in. Measure from the binding's center
fold twice the width of the finished
binding and mark with a pin.

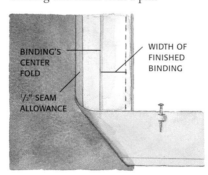

4 Fold binding back along pin mark,
right side in, and pin raw edge of
binding to bottom edge of curtain.
Draw a diagonal line across binding
from stitched seamline to crosswise
foldline. Reverse diagonal to point
where adjoining seams intersect. The
two diagonal lines should form a right
angle. Stitch along the marked line
through binding only. Trim excess
binding fabric along diagonal seams.

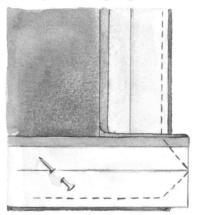

5 Finish pinning and then sew the
binding to bottom edge of curtain.
Turn binding to the wrong side and
slipstitch folded edge to the seamline.

SET-IN BANDING

This trimming is applied 4½ inches from the edge of the face fabric, allowing the face fabric to border the edge.

BANDING THAT ENDS AT THE LOWER EDGE OF THE FABRIC:

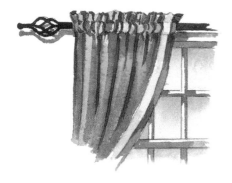

1 Cut a contrast strip the finished width plus 1 inch. Cut length is equal to the cut length of the face fabric.

2 Fold ½ inch to wrong side of one long edge; press. Measuring finished width from fold, press under seam allowance on other long edge.

3 Mark a guideline on right side of face fabric 4½ inches from leading edge. With band right side up and its ends aligned with top and bottom of curtain, pin leading edge of band to inside of guideline. Topstitch in place.

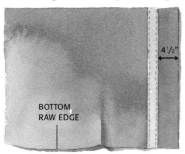

BOTTOM RAW EDGE

4½"

4 Make lower hems on face fabric. Attach lining as directed in project.

MITERED BANDING THAT CONTINUES ABOVE THE PANEL HEM:

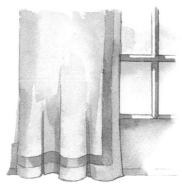

1 Determine finished width of band and how far from edge to place it. (A 2-inch-wide band set 4½ inches from leading edge and 4¼ inches from bottom—so band does not interfere with hem—is typical.)

Follow steps 1–2, "Banding that ends at the lower edge of the fabric," this page, to prepare contrast strip.

2 Make lower hems on face fabric and lining. Mark a line on face fabric 4½ inches from leading edge and 4¼ inches from lower hemline. Pin band to face fabric so leading edge of band aligns with marked line.

Topstitch inner edge of band, stopping a distance equal to finished width of band from the adjacent marked line.

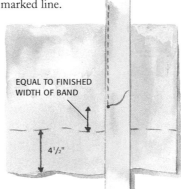

EQUAL TO FINISHED WIDTH OF BAND

4½"

3 Fold the band back on itself along the adjacent marked line. Draw a diagonal line from the corner to the last stitch on the inner edge; stitch along the diagonal line. Trim excess band along the seamline.

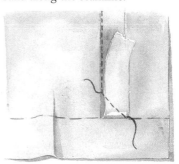

4 Continue sewing the inner edge of the band, pivoting at each corner.

5 Topstitch the leading edge of the band, pivoting at each corner; press.

flat panels

tab curtains

A tailored alternative to curtains with rings, tab curtains have a distinctly crisp, casual look.

TABS INSERTED IN LINED CURTAINS STEP-BY-STEP

1 Follow steps 1–6, "Lined flat panels," pages 40–41; do not sew the top edges together.

2 For tabs, drape a strip of fabric over rod. Pin and measure desired length; add 3 inches for two 1½-inch seam allowances to arrive at cut length (10 inches minimum). Finished width of tabs can vary (1½ to 2 inches is standard); add 1 inch for two ½-inch seam allowances to arrive at cut width.

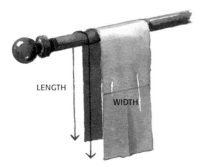

3 To figure number of spaces, subtract finished width of one tab from finished width of panel; divide by 6 inches (a trial space size) and round up to next whole number for number of spaces. (For example, for a 60-inch-wide finished panel with 2-inch-wide finished tabs, subtract 2 from 60 to get 58; divide by 6. Round result, 9.67, up to 10.)

To get actual space size, again subtract finished tab width from finished panel width and divide by number of spaces. (In example, divide 58 by 10 for a space size of 5.8, or 5¾ inches.)

Mark off spaces at top edge of face fabric, right side up, starting with a mark at half a tab width from each end of panel.

Number of tabs needed is equal to number of spaces plus 1.

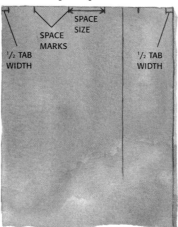

4 Cut lengthwise strips of fabric long enough so you can cut several tabs from each strip (this is easier and faster than stitching and turning each tab individually). Fold each strip in half lengthwise, right side in, and stitch the long edges together, using ½-inch seam allowance. Turn right side out and press so seam is at center. Cut required number of tabs. Fold each tab in half crosswise, seam on the inside.

5 Turn curtain wrong side out. Sandwich folded tabs, raw edges even with top edges of curtain and folds pointing down, between face fabric and lining, placing a tab against each side fold and centering remaining tabs over space marks. Sew across top edge through all thicknesses.

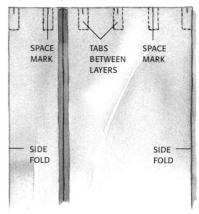

6 Turn curtain right side out and press. For added stability, topstitch 1¼ inches from top edge through all layers.

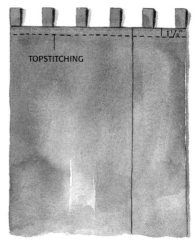

TABS TOPSTITCHED TO UNLINED CURTAINS STEP-BY-STEP

1 To determine the tab length, follow steps 2–3, "Tabs inserted in lined curtains," page 46, adding 3 inches total to cut length of each tab.

2 To make tabs, follow step 4, "Tabs inserted in lined curtains," page 46, but do not fold tabs in half. Turn each tab wrong side out; stitch across one end. Turn right side out and press.

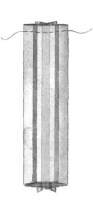

3 Follow steps 1–5, "Unlined flat panels," page 40.

4 Follow step 6, "Unlined flat panels," page 40. Before topstitching, insert unfinished ends of tabs ½ inch under hem turndown, aligning a tab with each side edge and centering remaining tabs over space marks. Topstitch close to the second fold.

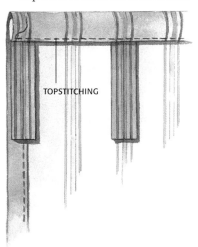

TOPSTITCHING

5 Bring tabs to the front of the curtain. Align finished ends 1½ inches below top of curtain. Topstitch a square on each tab, then add an X or other decorative stitch pattern.

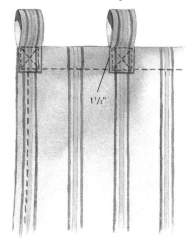

1½"

button tabs

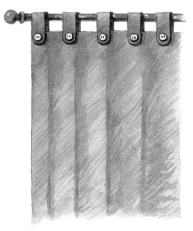

For a tailored look, button one end of the tab to the front of the curtain. Plan the tab length in the usual way, but curve or point the front end, figuring an overlap allowance equal to a bit more than the button diameter.

Follow instructions for attaching topstitched tabs to unlined curtains. Make a buttonhole in the finished end of each tab. Sew a button to the curtain opposite each folded-down tab.

knotted and bow-tied tabs

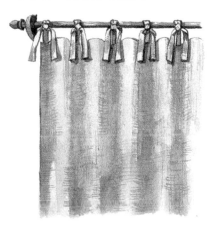

For tabs that are tied in knots or bows, experiment with strips of fabric tied and placed over the rod or pole, as in step 2, "Tabs inserted in lined curtains," page 46, to determine the length and width you'll need.

Instead of one looped tab, you'll need pairs of tabs. Turn each tab wrong side out and stitch across one end. Turn right side out and press. For tabs that are tied in bows on the curtain front, make the back tabs longer than the front tabs.

Stitch pairs of tabs to the top edge, following instructions for either lined or unlined curtain tab insertion.

making tiebacks

TIEBACKS hold treatments back from the window, shaping the treatment and letting in light. For a pair of tiebacks, you will need fabric, four 1/2-inch-diameter rings, and a pair of concealed tieback holders (or two cup hooks).

tailored tiebacks

For tailored tiebacks, you'll need two strips of heavy fusible interfacing.

1 To determine the finished size, wrap a tape measure gently around the curtain panel, bring the tape together, and swing it to the molding or wall where you'll attach a hook. A general rule of thumb is that a tailored tieback is half the rod length plus 4 inches (when laid flat).

2 Install concealed tieback holders into the wall or window trim or screw in cup hooks.

3 To determine the cut size, add 1 inch to the finished length; double the finished width and add 1 inch. For each tieback, cut one strip of fabric on the lengthwise grain and one strip of heavy fusible interfacing 1/2 inch smaller all around.

4 Center fusible interfacing on wrong side of tieback and fuse in place. Press short ends 1/2 inch to wrong side.

5 Fold strip in half lengthwise, right side in. Stitch long edges together, using 1/2-inch seam allowance.

6 Turn tieback right side out so lengthwise seam is face up and centered. Press. Turn pressed ends inside and slipstitch closed.

7 Leave ends square or press corners diagonally to inside to form a point and slipstitch in place. Hand-sew a ring to each end.

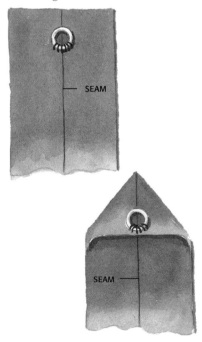

shaped tiebacks

Shaped tiebacks are a little more graceful than tailored tiebacks and fit the contour of the curtain fabric as it falls into place.

1 To make a pattern, cut a strip of medium-weight paper 4 to 6 inches wide and slightly longer than the tieback will be. Pin the paper around the curtain panel. Draw a curved shape and trim the paper, experimenting until you get the effect you want.

2 For each tieback, use the paper pattern to cut two pieces from fabric, adding a 1/2-inch seam allowance all around. Cut one piece from fusible interfacing without adding seam allowance. Fuse the interfacing to the wrong side of one fabric piece.

3 Place both pieces right sides together, and stitch all around with a ½-inch seam allowance. Leave an opening on one long edge for turning. Trim seams and clip curves.

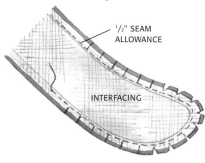

4 Turn tieback right side out and press. Slipstitch the opening closed. Hand-sew rings to each end at least ¼ inch from the edge.

shirred tiebacks

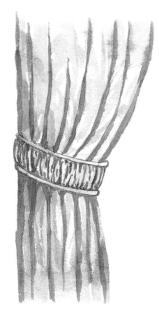

In addition to face fabric, you'll need lining, heavy fusible interfacing, and matching or contrasting welt; see Welting/piping" on page 29.

1 Follow steps 1–2, "Tailored tiebacks," page 48.

2 To determine the cut size, multiply finished length by 2 and add 2 inches; add 1 inch to finished width. For each tieback, cut one strip of fabric on lengthwise grain. For lining, add 2 inches to finished length and 1 inch to finished width; cut one lining strip. Cut one strip of fusible interfacing equal to finished length and width. Fuse to the wrong side of the lining.

3 Zigzag over a cord (button thread or crochet cotton) along each long edge. Pull the cords, gathering the strip to the finished length plus 2 inches. With raw edges aligned, baste welt to right side of tieback. Remove the welt cord in the seam allowances at each end to reduce bulk.

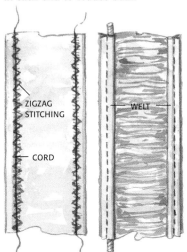

4 Pin lining to tieback, right sides together, and stitch close to welt, using previous stitching as a guide. Turn right side out.

5 Turn under 1 inch on each open end and slipstitch closed. Hand-sew rings to wrong side of tiebacks.

tied sash

A long band of fabric wrapped around the curtain and tied in a bow or knot is a simple and often very effective tieback. Your choice of fabric and the way you tie it makes a sash elegant, casual, or whimsical.

To determine the sash length, tie a scarf or ribbon around the curtain and make a bow; then measure the length of the scarf or ribbon.

Cut and sew the sash and tack a ring to the middle of the sash. Place the ring over the hook on the window trim. Wrap and tie the sash around the curtain.

making tiebacks

jumbo welt tiebacks

Plump cord ¾ inch or more in diameter gives jumbo welt tiebacks their soft, oversize look. Choose a cord size appropriate to the scale of the treatment. With this method, you'll have leftover cord.

1 For two tiebacks, cut a length of cord equal to four times the finished length of one tieback plus 4 inches. Cut a strip of fabric equal to twice the finished length of one tieback plus 2 inches, and 1 inch wider than the cord circumference. If piecing is necessary, try to position seam at the midpoint.

2 Starting at midpoint of cord, wrap strip of fabric around cord, right side in, aligning raw edges. Using a zipper foot, stitch down long edge of fabric close to cord (don't crowd cord). Hand-stitch securely across the starting point.

MIDPOINT

HAND-STITCHING

3 Pull end of cord free from open end of casing and hold securely. Turn open end of fabric over itself; push casing over itself until fabric tube is right side out over cord.

MIDPOINT

RIGHT SIDE OF FABRIC

Cut off uncovered portion of cord. Cut fabric-covered portion of cord in half for two tiebacks.

4 To finish ends, trim out ½ inch of cord; turn casing to inside and sew closed. Sew rings to the ends.

knotted welt tiebacks

To determine finished length of one tieback, tie a decorative knot in a length of cord and with it tie back a panel, adjusting length and height until effect is pleasing. Mark desired finished length on cord; remove, untie, and measure.

Make two jumbo welt tiebacks to this length. Make a decorative knot near center of each before installing.

shirred welt tiebacks

For each tieback, cut a fabric strip 2 times the tieback length and 2 inches wider than the circumference of the cord. Follow the method for turning jumbo welt tiebacks to encase the cord, shirring the fabric over the cord as the tube is turned. Finish ends; attach rings.

braided welt tiebacks

For one tieback, cut cord 9 times the tieback length plus 4 inches. Cut fabric 4½ times the length of tieback. Follow the method for turning jumbo welt tiebacks to encase the cord. Cut covered cord into three equal sections.

To make a braid with three different fabrics, make three separate cords, each one twice the finished length plus 2 inches. (For a one-color braid it may also be easier to make three individual cords than to turn a single long cord.)

Turn ends of all three pieces to the inside; slipstitch. Overlap the three cords slightly at one end and hand-sew them together. Braid the cords; when braid reaches desired tieback length, cut off excess cord. Slipstitch to finish. Attach rings.

tieback hardware

Decorative hardware and accessories are sometimes used instead of fabric tiebacks to secure draped panels. Holdbacks are available in a wide variety of styles and finishes. They can match the drapery rod style or be design elements on their own. From metal to plastic to iron, tieback holders with projection arms or stems hold fabric back casually. Hook style holdbacks hold the fabric more securely.

Fabric tiebacks can be attached to concealed tieback holders, which prevent the drapery from being crushed. Cup hooks and 1¼-inch tieback hooks hold fabric tiebacks at the sides of windows. Tieback rings in plastic or metal are sewn to the back of the tieback.

sophisticated tiebacks

Whether you repeat the curtain or drapery materials, add a contrast, or introduce an embellishment, you have numerous options for tieback design. Here are more ideas for giving a special finish to your window treatment design.

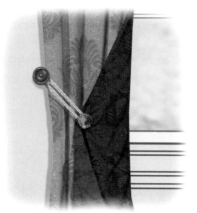

A cord loop extending from a button to a holdback reveals the contrasting drapery lining.

A soft choux rosette complements the gathered fabric of a narrow ruched tieback.

Fake fruit added to a cloth tieback brings a bit of whimsy to short kitchen curtains.

Wire-edged ribbon tied into a big multiloop bow holds its shape well.

Diagonally folded fabric wrapped with cord makes an unusual tieback.

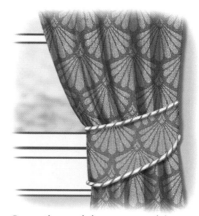

Decorative cord dresses up a plain, contoured tieback.

A double-cord tieback with two big tassels adds a classic, elegant finish.

Ruffled tiebacks are the perfect accompaniment to ruffled curtains.

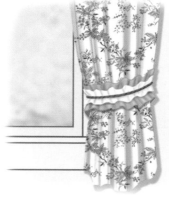

Accent a small, two-layer, double-ruffle tieback with decorative cord.

rod-pocket curtains

SOFT AND TRADITIONAL, this basic curtain style can be installed on a flat or round rod or pole of any size. You can make them with or without a heading; the instructions cover both. A heading above the pocket forms an instant ruffle as the rod is inserted.

A simple trick for softening the top of a rod-pocket curtain is to sew a heading twice as deep as you would like it to appear at the window. Then, after slipping the rod or pole through the pocket, separate the two layers of fabric to pouf the heading.

ROD-POCKET CHART

The rod pocket must be large enough to accommodate the rod or pole comfortably and to allow the curtain to gather on the rod. Following are rod-pocket sizes for standard rods; use the appropriate pocket size when calculating yardage.

ROD TYPE	ROD DIAMETER	POCKET SIZE
SASH OR FLAT	UP TO 3/4"	1 1/2"
ROUND	UP TO 1"	2 1/4"
	UP TO 1 1/2"	3 1/4"
	UP TO 2"	4 1/4"
	UP TO 3"	5 1/2"
WIDE	2 1/2"	3 1/2"
	4 1/2"	5 1/2"

CALCULATING YARDAGE

Measure your window and fill in the window treatment work sheet (see pages 14–18). For most curtains, a fullness of 2 1/2 times the finished width is best. If your fabric is sheer, multiply finished width by 3. You'll need extra fabric for the tiebacks (see pages 48–52).

Use the following allowances in your calculations:

LOWER HEMS	0"
SIDE HEMS	6" TOTAL
TOP	2 × POCKET + 2 × HEADING (IF USED)

UNLINED ROD-POCKET CURTAINS STEP-BY-STEP

1 Choose and prepare fabric, and join the fabric widths (see pages 21–26). Press seams open.

2 Fold and stitch lower hems (see page 27).

3 Fold and stitch side hems (see page 28).

4 On right side of fabric, measure from lower edge a distance equal to finished length. Mark with pins every 4 inches across panel.

5 Measure and mark proper top allowance (2 times pocket plus 2 times heading, if used) above finished-length line. Trim ravel allowance.

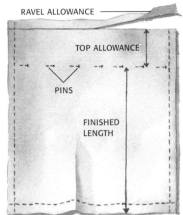

6 Fold down top edge, wrong side in, along finished-length line; press. Remove pins. Turn raw edge in to meet pressed fold and press again. Stitch close to second fold. For heading, if used, stitch again from top fold a distance equal to heading depth; press.

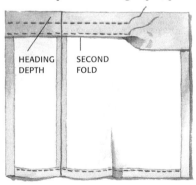

7 Slip rod through pocket between back two layers of fabric, gathering fabric evenly.

LINED ROD-POCKET CURTAIN STEP-BY-STEP

Use the following allowances in your calculations for the lining:

LOWER HEMS	4"
SIDE HEMS	NONE
TOP	NONE

1 Follow steps 1–2, 4–5, "Unlined rod-pocket curtains," page 53.

2 Cut lining 3 inches longer than the finished length of curtain and 6 inches narrower than cut width of curtain; allow for joining seams to align on face fabric and lining. Sew together widths for each layer; press.

3 Turn, press, and stitch 2-inch double lower hem on the lining. With right sides together, pin lining to face fabric so edges are aligned at one side and lower hemmed edge of lining is 1 inch above lower hemmed edge of curtain. Lining ends at top fold line. Stitch 1½-inch-wide seam. Repeat on other side and press seam allowances toward face fabric.

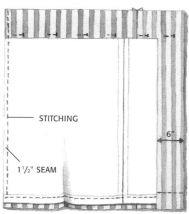

STITCHING

1½" SEAM

6"

4 To complete the curtain, follow steps 6–7, "Unlined rod-pocket curtains," page 53.

rod sleeve

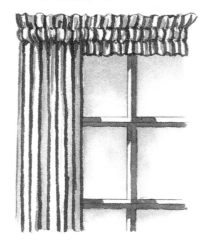

When rod-pocket curtains don't meet in the center but just hang at the sides of the window, a simple sleeve that fits on the rod between the panels visually bridges the gap and completes the treatment.

If the panels on either side have a heading, give the rod sleeve the same heading. For a custom look, add another heading below the rod pocket.

CALCULATING YARDAGE

The following method of determining yardage gives even fullness across the rod.

1 Multiply rod length by 2½ and subtract the finished width (flat measurement) of side panels. Divide remainder by usable fabric width and round to the nearest whole number to arrive at number of widths needed for sleeve.

2 The cut length (up-and-down measurement) is equal to 2 times rod pocket plus 2 times heading depth for each heading, if used, plus 1 inch. For patterned fabric, calculate repeat cut length (see page 18). Try to match the pattern horizontally on sleeve and curtain pockets.

3 Multiply cut length or repeat cut length by number of widths and divide by 36 inches for yards needed.

ROD SLEEVE STEP-BY-STEP

1 Join fabric widths as described on page 26. Press seams open.

2 Make a ½-inch hem on each end. Fold fabric in half lengthwise, right side in. Pin and stitch long edges together, using ½-inch seam allowance. Turn right side out. Center seam at back and press.

3 For a single heading, if used, stitch from top fold a distance equal to heading depth; for a double heading, if used, stitch parallel to both folds at a distance equal to heading depth.

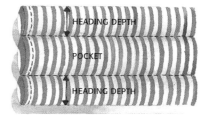

HEADING DEPTH

POCKET

HEADING DEPTH

4 Slip rod through pocket, gathering fabric evenly.

sophisticated ruffles

Depending on their fabric and proportions, ruffles can be elegant, sophisticated, quirky, crisp, or—of course—soft and sweet. They may match or contrast with the rest of the window treatment, be single or multilayered, pleated or gathered with or without a heading, and may be embellished with trim. They follow a curve well, so they're a good choice for shaped edges.

A very deep, gathered ruffle drapes softly from the edge of a curtain.

A two-layer, gathered ruffle of moderate depth adds a jaunty frill.

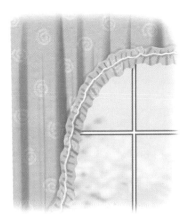

A small ruffle with a petite heading works especially well along curves.

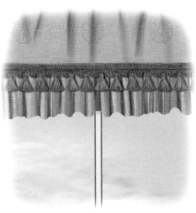

A gathered ruffle gains sophistication when topped by tassel fringe.

A deep sawtooth gives an intriguing finish to a frill of crisp fabric.

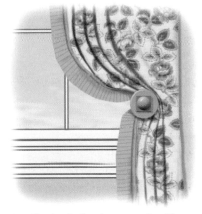

Small, crisp knife pleats march with poised precision along a drapery edge.

A shallow, inverted pleat ruffle springs open with crisp dimension.

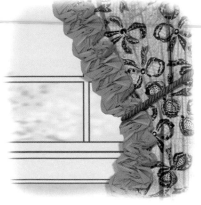

A serpentine ruffle creates a double scallop embellishment.

sash curtain

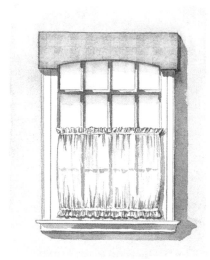

Gathered and stretched on two rods, an unlined sash curtain is a good choice for a casement window or a French door—the lower rod keeps the curtain in place when the window or door is opened or closed. This style of curtain works on a door with a small inset window and on the bottom sash of a double-hung window as well. A sash curtain can be made either with or without headings.

CALCULATING YARDAGE

Measure your window and fill in the window treatment work sheet (see pages 14–18). For most sash curtains, a fullness of 2½ times the finished width is best. If you are using a sheer fabric, multiply the finished width by 3.

Use the following allowances in your calculations. Remember that you need a pocket (and a heading, if used) at both top and bottom. Refer to the top chart on page 53 for pocket size.

TOP AND BOTTOM	2 × POCKET + 2 × HEADING (IF USED)
SIDE HEMS	6" TOTAL

SASH CURTAIN STEP-BY-STEP

1 Choose and prepare fabric. Join the fabric widths and finish seams (see pages 21–26).

2 Fold and stitch side hems (see page 28).

3 Turn up lower edge, wrong side in, a distance equal to bottom allowance; press. Turn raw edge in to meet pressed fold and press again. Stitch as you did side hems; press. For the bottom heading, if used, stitch from the lower fold a distance equal to the heading depth.

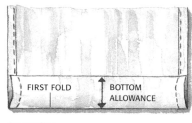

FIRST FOLD   BOTTOM ALLOWANCE

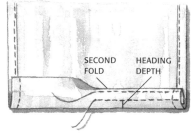

SECOND FOLD   HEADING DEPTH

4 On right side of face fabric, measure from lower edge a distance equal to finished length and mark with pins every 4 inches across panel.

5 Measure and mark proper top allowances (2 times pocket plus 2 times heading, if used) above the pin-marked finished-length line. Trim the ravel allowance.

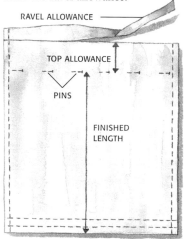

RAVEL ALLOWANCE

TOP ALLOWANCE

PINS

FINISHED LENGTH

6 Fold down top edge, wrong side in, along finished-length line; press. Remove pins. Turn raw edge in to meet pressed fold and press again. For top heading, if used, stitch again from top fold a distance equal to the heading depth.

7 Slip rods through pockets between back two layers of fabric, gathering fabric evenly. Install top rod, and then bottom rod, so curtain is taut.

hourglass curtain

A close cousin to the sash curtain, the hourglass style evokes a range of decorating moods depending on the fabric chosen.

Because of the tension on the curtain, the curtain must be at least a third longer than the rod length. (If, for example, your rod is 24 inches, the curtain must be at least 32 inches long.) Any curtain closer to square than this won't stay in the hourglass configuration.

CALCULATING YARDAGE

Measure your window and fill in the window treatment work sheet (see pages 14–18). For most hourglass curtains, a fullness of 2½ times the finished width is best. If you are using a sheer fabric, multiply the finished width by 3.

Use the following allowances in your calculations. Remember that you need a pocket (and a heading, if used) at both top and bottom. Allow additional fabric for a tieback and, if desired, a rosette. Refer to the top chart on page 53 for pocket size.

TOP AND BOTTOM	2 × POCKET + 2 × HEADING (IF USED)
SIDE HEMS	6" TOTAL
STRETCH ALLOWANCE	4"

1 Choose and prepare fabric. Join the fabric widths and finish seams (see pages 21–26).

2 Fold and stitch side hems (see page 28).

3 Fold fabric panel in half crosswise, lining up side seams, and press fold at center. Fold panel lengthwise and press again at center. Mark center point where folds intersect with a safety pin or use a fabric marker.

4 Measure from center point toward top a distance equal to half the finished length; measure and mark the same distance from center point toward the bottom. Mark with pins every 4 inches across panel.

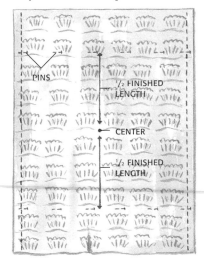

5 At side hems, add 2 inches to pinned lines at both top and bottom and mark these points. (Finished length of panel is now 4 inches more at edges than at center.) At top and bottom, draw a gentle curve from marks at side edges to center to mark new finished-length line.

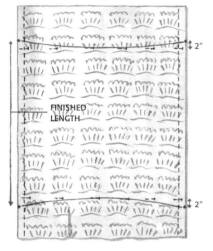

6 At a distance equal to top and bottom allowance (2 times pocket plus 2 times heading, if used), draw another curve at top and bottom parallel to the first. Cut on second curved lines; remove pins.

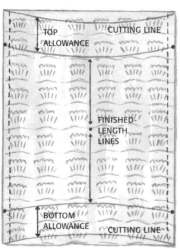

7 Fold down top edge, wrong side in, along curved finished-length line; press. Turn raw edge in to meet pressed fold and press again. Stitch close to second fold. For heading, if used, stitch again from top fold a distance equal to heading depth. Repeat for lower pocket.

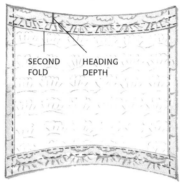

8 Slip sash rods into rod pockets between back two layers of fabric, gathering fabric evenly. Mount curtain, installing top rod first and then bottom rod so curtain is taut in center.

9 To determine size of tieback, pull panel into hourglass shape at center and tie with string or scrap fabric (make sure side hems are straight and ends of rods are covered). Add 2 inches for overlap to arrive at finished length of tieback and add 1 inch for seam allowances. The finished width should be between 2 and 3 inches; double that figure and add 1 inch for seam allowances.

10 To make tieback, see pages 48–51. To make a rosette or other embellishment, see pages 136–138.

sunburst curtain

A sunburst curtain is actually a type of sash curtain. The top pocket is gathered over a curved flexible rod and the lower hem is pulled through a ring installed at the bottom center of a semicircular window. Choose a lightweight or sheer fabric for this style, and when possible, railroad the fabric to avoid seams.

This curtain works best if the window's radius is 36 inches or less; on a window larger than that, you'll have too much fabric at the center. Also, because a sunburst curtain relies on equal tension from the center out to the curve, you'll get the best results on half-circle windows. Don't use a sunburst curtain on an elliptical window if the difference between the window's height and the radius at the base is greater than 6 inches.

Hang the curtain on a flexible clear rod supported with brackets. You'll also need a wood drapery ring with an eyelet to form the rosette and a cup hook to secure the ring.

CALCULATING YARDAGE

Refer to the drawing below as you measure.

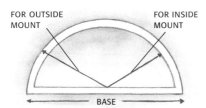

1 For number of fabric widths, measure window's finished width, or curve, and multiply by 2 for the fullness; add 6 inches for side hems. For fabric that runs vertically, divide this figure by usable fabric width. If railroading fabric, divide figure by 36 inches to determine the yards needed.

2 To find finished length, divide base of window by 2 and add 3 inches to allow for rosette; for an outside mount, add coverage beyond opening. For top allowance on an inside or outside mount, add 5 inches total for a 1½-inch pocket and a 1-inch heading (a heading is recommended even on an inside mount to ensure a snug fit). Add 6 inches for hem at base.

3 For fabric that runs vertically, multiply cut length by number of widths and divide by 36 inches for yards needed.

SUNBURST CURTAIN STEP-BY-STEP

1 Choose and prepare fabric. Join the fabric widths and finish the seams (see pages 21–27).

2 Fold and stitch side hems (see page 28).

3 Turn up lower hem 6 inches, wrong side in, and press. Turn raw edge in to meet pressed fold and press again. Stitch close to second fold.

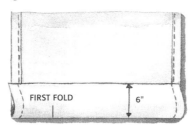

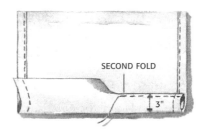

4 On right side of fabric, measure from lower hem a distance equal to finished length plus 3 inches for finished-length line; mark with pins every 4 inches across panel. Measure and mark 5 inches beyond pin-marked line. Trim ravel allowance.

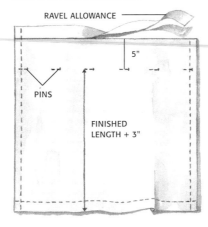

5 Fold top, wrong side in, on finished-length line; press. Remove pins. Turn raw edge in to meet pressed fold and press again. Stitch close to second fold. For heading, stitch again 1 inch from top fold.

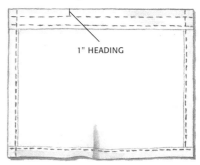

6 Slip rod through pocket, adjusting gathers evenly, and mount. To make rosette, gather lower edge in your hand and pull through ring.

7 For an outside mount, screw in a cup hook below center point of window. Turn hook sideways, slip eyelet over, and turn hook down. For an inside mount, screw hook into sill; slip eyelet over hook.

8 Arrange fabric for rosette to conceal ring. You may tack it in place with a needle and thread, or use a rubber band to secure the shape.

draperies

BELOW: *Here, rectangular pinch-pleat draperies hanging on a discreet rod mounted above an arched window are pulled all the way off the window—something not possible with arch shaped panels, which can't open to show the top of the window. Fabric the same color as the wall makes these unobtrusive.*

TOP RIGHT: *Crisp pinch-pleat draperies team easily with Venetian blinds; this ensemble shares the honey tones of the wallpaper and furnishings.*

RIGHT: *Sheer pinch-pleat draperies hung from the ceiling over a window wall look thoroughly modern; they're sophisticated and not at all stuffy.*

A coordinating border topped with tassel fringe accents these pinch-pleat drapes, which are made from a simple, fairly crisp, figured silk fabric and hung from rings on a decorative pole. A wide, sheer Roman shade hangs behind them, spanning a set of casement windows.

how to make draperies

WHAT WAS ONCE the mainstay of window fashions—the pinch-pleated drapery—continues as a favorite for formal decors and is sometimes made in sheer or informal fabric for more casual settings. Five styles of pinch pleats are offered here. Your choice of concealed or decorative rod also plays a role in the overall look.

drapery hardware

Rods and accessories range from plain conventional traverse rods to more decorative rods with interesting details. Department stores, home improvement centers, and large fabric stores carry hardware made by a handful of manufacturers. Consult mail-order sources or an interior designer to see more diverse styles.

RODS AND BRACKETS

Standard for draperies is the traverse rod, which allows you to open and close the panels by pulling a cord that moves small slides along a track.

An adjustable *conventional traverse rod* is designed to be concealed when the treatment is closed. The drapery hooks on the leading edge of each panel fit into master slides, which overlap at the center of the rod.

For sliding glass doors, use a one-way draw rod. On a bay window, try placing a one-way rod at each side and a two-way rod at the center.

Decorative traverse rods, which range in style from contemporary to traditional, are exposed whether the drapery is open or closed. Most of these rods come with half round ring-slide combinations and with finials that attach to the ends.

End brackets can be decorative or plain. Most decorative brackets are adjustable and visible; they support the rod from underneath. Plain ones are adjustable and placed at the ends of a conventional traverse rod, hidden from view by the draperies.

Support brackets, also adjustable, ease some of the strain on long drapery rods. As a rule, you'll need one for every 40 inches of rod length.

NOTIONS AND ACCESSORIES

You'll find these items in the notions section of fabric and decorating stores.

Four-inch-wide *crinoline* (often called buckram) stiffens the headings on pleated draperies. Crinoline comes in woven and nonwoven types.

Drapery hooks, available 1 and 1¼ inches long, are designed to sit in the slides of a traverse rod without shifting under the weight of the fabric. The standard 1¼-inch hook is used in most professional workrooms. The smaller 1-inch hook is sometimes used in sheer and lightweight fabrics.

Drapery weights sewn into the corners of the lower hem assure that panels will hang straight.

Decorative holdbacks and *concealed tieback holders* are sometimes used with draperies. For photos, see page 51.

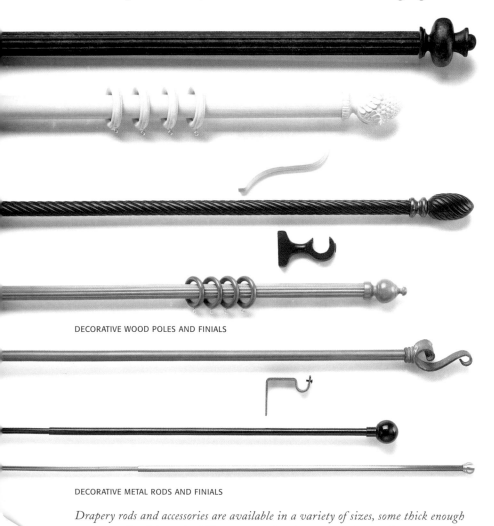

DECORATIVE WOOD POLES AND FINIALS

DECORATIVE METAL RODS AND FINIALS

Drapery rods and accessories are available in a variety of sizes, some thick enough to support lined draperies. The accompanying brackets are larger also.

hardware installation

Read the manufacturer's instructions from beginning to end before you install a drapery rod. Having a helper will make the installation easier.

ROD PLACEMENT

Refer to your window treatment worksheet (page 16) for the distance above window to hang the drapery top.

For a conventional traverse rod, set the top of the brackets at a height equal to the finished length of the drapery, allowing for the panels to hang ½ inch above the floor.

For a decorative rod, follow the manufacturer's instructions to find the prescribed distance from the top of the drapery heading to the top screw hole on the brackets.

HOW TO MOUNT RODS

Here's the usual installation sequence.

1 Mount the end brackets and support brackets, if used. Use a carpenter's level to check the position of the brackets. Mark through the screw holes.

2 Mount a conventional rod by slipping it over the end brackets. For a decorative rod, arrange the rings before you tighten the brackets. For either rod, adjust the clips on any support brackets so they fit snugly over the rod.

3 Adjust the cord, mount the tension pulley, and center the master slide. Add or remove the slides or ring-slides so you have the correct number for your drapery hooks. Cut the cord only after you're sure you've allowed enough length to pull the panels shut.

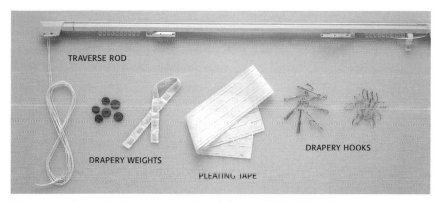

TRAVERSE ROD

DRAPERY WEIGHTS

PLEATING TAPE

DRAPERY HOOKS

Drapery notions include a traverse rod, weights available either singly or sewn into a tape, pleating tape, and drapery hooks in several sizes.

hanging draperies

With the master slides near the center but not overlapping, start hanging one panel by inserting the first two hooks on the return edge into the holes on the bracket. Insert the remaining hooks into the slides, ending with the master slide. Repeat for the other panel.

TRAINING DRAPERIES

After they are hung, train your draperies so the pleats are uniform.

Open the panels completely. Then arrange them with your fingers, pulling the pleats forward and pushing back the fabric in between. Gently tie the panel near the top and bottom with fabric strips. Leave for several days to set the folds.

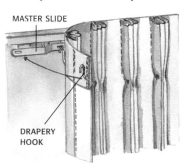

MASTER SLIDE

DRAPERY HOOK

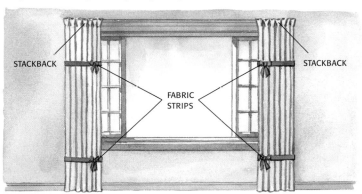

STACKBACK

STACKBACK

FABRIC STRIPS

pinch pleats

PINCH-PLEATED DRAPERIES and their close relatives (see the variations on pages 66–67) are versatile treatments that offer a range of looks, from classic traditional to modern. Pinch pleats are sometimes called French pleats.

The directions that follow are for a single lined panel (for an unlined version, see page 66). At each end of the panel and at every pleat, you'll need a pin-on drapery hook. For stiffener, use 4-inch-wide crinoline. If you're making two panels for a window, remember that they must be mirror images of each other.

CALCULATING YARDAGE

Measure your window and fill in the window treatment work sheet (see pages 14–18). Draperies have returns and overlaps; fullness is usually $2\frac{1}{2}$ times finished width. Most draperies begin at the top of the window casing and end $\frac{1}{2}$ inch above floor level.

Use the following allowances in your calculations:

	FABRIC	LINING
LOWER HEM	8"	4"
SIDE HEMS	6" TOTAL	NONE
TOP	8"	NONE

PINCH PLEATS STEP-BY-STEP

1 Choose and prepare face fabric and lining, and join the fabric widths (see pages 21–26). Press seams open.

2 Fold and stitch lower hems (see page 27).

3 On wrong side of face fabric, measure from lower hem a distance equal to finished length and mark with pins every 4 inches across panel.

4 Lay lining on face fabric, right sides together, so that lower edge of lining is 1 inch above the lower edge of face fabric. Starting from leading edge, align first seam of the face fabric with first seam of the lining.

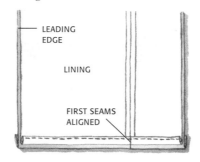

LEADING EDGE

LINING

FIRST SEAMS ALIGNED

5 Trim face fabric or lining if needed so lining is 3 inches narrower than face fabric on each side.

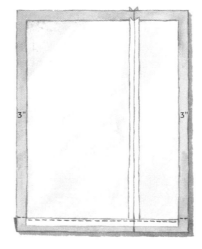

3"   3"

6 Trim lining so upper edge meets pin-marked finished-length line on face fabric. Then, on face fabric, measure and mark 8-inch top allowance above finished-length line. Trim ravel allowance.

RAVEL ALLOWANCE

TOP ALLOWANCE

FINISHED LENGTH

7 Pin lining to face fabric, right sides together, so that leading edge of lining is aligned with the leading edge of face fabric (lining hem should still be 1 inch above face fabric hem). Starting at lower edge and continuing to top, sew together using $1\frac{1}{2}$-inch seam allowance.

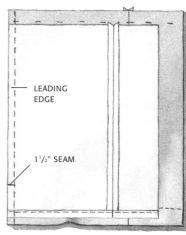

LEADING EDGE

$1\frac{1}{2}$" SEAM

8 Separate face fabric from lining, laying both right sides down. Press seam allowances toward face fabric.

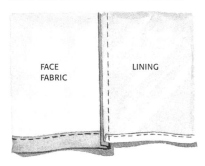

FACE FABRIC

LINING

Turn lining and face fabric wrong sides together, so 1¹/₂ inches of face fabric shows on back and seam allowance is tucked into fold; press.

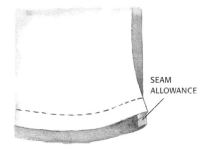

SEAM ALLOWANCE

9 With right sides together, align other side edges of lining and face fabric. Pin and stitch as in step 7. Turn panel right side out. Fold seam toward return edge as in step 8 so 1¹/₂ inches of face fabric shows at each side; press.

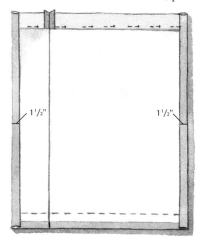

1¹/₂"   1¹/₂"

10 Fold one end of crinoline under 1 inch; place fold ¹/₄ inch from edge of panel, aligning lower edge of crinoline with finished-length line; pin. Pin crinoline across panel to opposite side. Trim end and fold under 1 inch, positioning fold ¹/₄ inch from edge. Remove pins from finished-length line.

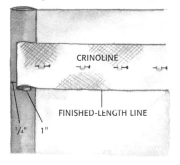

CRINOLINE

FINISHED-LENGTH LINE

¹/₄"   1"

11 Fold 4-inch allowance over crinoline, press edge, and remove pins. Fold and press again; pin in place.

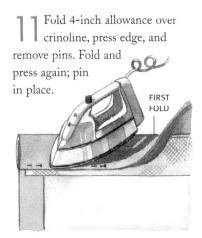

FIRST FOLD

12 Stitch side of heading closed, ¹/₈ inch from edge; backstitch. Stitch again, 1³/₈ inches from edge.

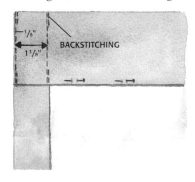

¹/₈"
BACKSTITCHING
1³/₈"

13 *For a single-panel treatment,* subtract the width of finished drapery from the width of flat panel. *For each panel of a two-panel treatment,* subtract half of finished drapery width from width of flat panel. Record result.

14 Multiply number of full fabric widths in each panel by 5 and half-widths by 2 to find number of pleats per panel. Number of spaces will be one less than number of pleats.

15 To determine pleat width, divide result from step 13 by number of pleats (step 14). Round off to nearest ¹/₄ inch.

16 To determine space between pleats, subtract return (figured previously) and 3¹/₂ inches for overlap from finished width. Divide by the number of spaces between pleats (step 14). Round off to nearest ¹/₄ inch.

17 Starting at the leading edge, measure in 3¹/₂ inches; place a pin through top edge to indicate start of first pleat. Measure and pin to mark end of pleat and then measure and mark space to beginning of next pleat.

Continue, marking all pleats and spaces; the space after the last pleat should equal the return measurement. Adjust pins slightly, if necessary, so last pleat ends where return begins.

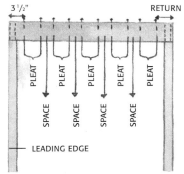

3¹/₂"   RETURN

PLEAT PLEAT PLEAT PLEAT PLEAT

SPACE SPACE SPACE SPACE

LEADING EDGE

pinch pleats

If fabric widths have been joined to make panel, adjust all pins so seams fall close to edge of pleats. Don't alter size of space; make adjustments in pleats only.

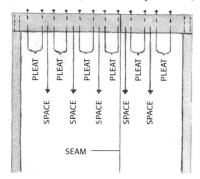

18 On wrong side of heading, bring together pins at sides of pleats. Lightly finger-press folds.

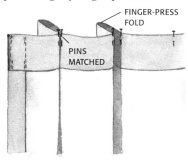

PINS MATCHED

FINGER-PRESS FOLD

Stitch pleats from bottom of the crinoline to top of panel at the point where pins meet; backstitch at each end. Push down on each side of each crease to form two more loops, making sure all three are even.

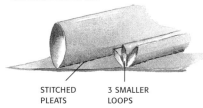

STITCHED PLEATS

3 SMALLER LOOPS

19 Drop the feed dogs on the sewing machine and zigzag a tack stitch ½ inch from bottom of crinoline in the center of the pleat through all layers.

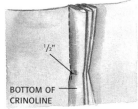

½"

BOTTOM OF CRINOLINE

20 To determine insertion point for drapery hooks, see chart below. Decorative rods may vary; check manufacturer's instructions.

TYPE OF ROD	INSERTION POINT	
	1" HOOK	1¼" HOOK
CONVENTIONAL (The top of the hook should be 2" from the top of the drapery.)	3"	3¼"
DECORATIVE (The top of the hook should be ½" from the top of the drapery.)	1½"	1¾"

Pin a drapery hook to the back of each pleat, to the end of the return, and ¾ inch from the leading edge so it pierces the crinoline but not the face fabric.

21 To give crinoline "memory," crease it vertically at midpoint between pleats; crease forward for a traverse rod, back for a decorative rod.

UNLINED PINCH PLEATS

Draperies made from casement and sheer fabrics are not lined, and some casual draperies made in opaque fabrics are also unlined. Use the same side, hem, and top allowances for unlined pinch-pleated draperies as for lined draperies. The side hems are constructed as you would when making unlined curtains (see page 28).

goblet pleats

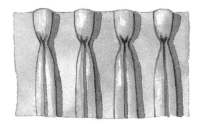

Goblet pleats are an elegant drapery heading that crushes easily, so use only for stationary treatments.

1 Follow steps 1–17, "Pinch pleats," pages 64–66, to make the panels and pin-mark the pleats.

2 On wrong side of heading, bring together pins at sides of pleat. Stitch pleat from bottom of crinoline to top of panel at point where pins meet. Backstitch at each end.

3 At base of each pleat, make tucks and hand-tack just above lower edge of crinoline.

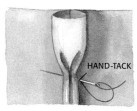

HAND-TACK

4 Open top of pleat, forming a round goblet shape. Hand-tack back of each goblet to top of panel on either side of vertical stitching.

HAND-TACKING

5 Insert drapery hooks. See step 20, "Pinch pleats," on this page.

6 Slip a roll of crinoline into each goblet to maintain shape.

butterfly pleats

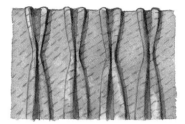

Two rather than three folds in each pleat distinguish the butterfly pleat from the basic pinch pleat.

1 Follow steps 1–17, "Pinch pleats," pages 64–66, to make the panels and pin-mark the pleats.

2 Follow step 2, "Goblet pleats," page 66, to stitch pleats.

3 Center each pleat over vertical stitching and flatten.

4 Bring folded edges together and, making sure they're even, finger-press two pleats.

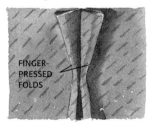

FINGER-PRESSED FOLDS

5 To finish, follow steps 19–21, "Pinch pleats," page 66.

pencil pleats

Pleating tape sewn to the back of a drapery panel is used to achieve this pleat style. By pulling the cords inside the tape, you can gather the heading into even, narrow, pencil-size pleats.

Select either 3-inch or 4-inch pencil-pleat drapery shirring tape. The shirring tape substitutes for crinoline. Allow a 1½-inch top allowance.

1 Follow steps 1–9, "Pinch pleats," pages 64–65.

2 Fold down the top allowance to the wrong side and press.

3 Pin shirring tape ¼ inch down from top of panel. Pull out ½ inch of each cord at each end; turn tape under at ends. Stitch tape along top, bottom, and between rows of cord.

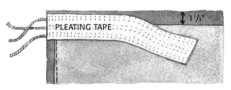

PLEATING TAPE

1½"

4 Knot ends of tape along one edge. Apply glue to knots to keep in place. Trim ends.

5 Pull other ends of cords until panel gathers up to finished width. Knot, glue, and trim pulled cord ends. Insert drapery hooks. See step 20, "Pinch pleats," page 66.

reverse pinch pleats

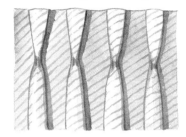

Sleek reverse pinch pleats are folded to the back.

1 Follow steps 1–17, "Pinch pleats," pages 64–66, to make the panels and pin-mark the pleats.

2 Follow step 2, "Goblet pleats," page 66, to stitch pleats.

3 Center each pleat over vertical stitching and gently flatten.

4 Roll folded edges around to touch stitching.

5 Hand-tack pleats just above lower edge of crinoline, placing stitches at back of each pleat and just catching folded edges.

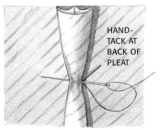

HAND-TACK AT BACK OF PLEAT

6 Insert drapery hooks. See step 20, "Pinch pleats," page 66.

shades

RIGHT: *When Roman shades that are rigged only at the sides are raised, their lower edge drapes in a wide, soft scallop. This pair is made from a large-scale gingham and flanked by plain curtains.*

BELOW: *Cloud shades that have a dowel in the hem fall in even poufs when raised. This example is made like a rod pocket curtain instead of being gathered with shirring tape and is inside-mounted in a deep-set window.*

shades

This striking London shade variant features a full pleat at the center and a half pleat near each edge; it falls in two poufs instead of the usual one. Its fabrication couldn't be simpler—unpatterned, rich red fabric trimmed with matching tassel fringe.

A set of soft, skirted Roman shades makes a discreet covering for a wall of full-length windows. Each shade is rigged at the sides and in the center so it swags in two gentle poufs. The skirt is simply the area above the bottom hem, which is left to hang flat instead of being connected to the rigging.

ABOVE: *These tailed cloud shades vary in width to suit their respective windows. Because they're made without bottom dowels, they fall in deep scallops that show off the coordinated small ruffle edging.*

LEFT: *Balloon shades are pleated rather than gathered at the top; they create a more restrained, tailored effect than their exuberant cloud shade cousins.*

ABOVE LEFT: *A scalloped roller shade trimmed with contrast fabric adds a dressy finish under plain curtains.*

ABOVE RIGHT: *The front of a soft-fold Roman shade falls in regular horizontal pleats even when it is lowered. This one is trimmed with brush fringe.*

RIGHT: *Bright, boldly figured fabric brings drama to even the simplest, plain, crisp Roman shades. These are inside-mounted in deep windows.*

OPPOSITE: *Because they're easy to adapt to various sizes, Roman shades are a good choice for ganged windows. This outside-mounted set features self-valances; the wide shade on the taller middle window is rigged to drape softly and is flanked by smaller versions.*

how to make shades

SHADES ARE as practical as they are good-looking—they control light, provide insulation, and ensure privacy. Use them alone or team them with curtains, draperies, valances, or cornices.

It's best to line Roman, balloon, and cloud shades; they hang better and the lining protects the face fabric from sun damage. And, as with other treatments, a lining provides a bit of insulation.

inside or outside mount?

An inside-mounted shade fits between the frame on either side of the window and ends at the sill. For Roman, balloon, and cloud shades, the finished width of the shade is the width of the window opening less ¹/₂ inch.

An outside-mounted shade's finished width will be the width of the area you decide to cover. The lower rod comes to the sill, with the skirt or permanent pouf, if used, covering the apron or extending below the window opening.

For an inside- or outside-mounted roller shade, the finished width of the shade will be the same as the length of the roller itself (not including the roller hardware).

hardware and notions

Roman, balloon, and cloud shades use the same basic materials; roller shades require their own hardware. For a look at shade hardware, see photo below.

ROMAN, BALLOON, AND CLOUD SHADE HARDWARE

To make any of these shades, you'll need specialized notions from shops that carry shade and drapery supplies, as well as some general hardware store items.

Supplies for rigging the shade include ¹/₄- or ¹/₂-inch rings, Roman shade cord or lightweight traverse cord, a shade pull, screw eyes, a small awning or shade cleat, and a ³/₈-inch-diameter sash curtain rod, brass rod, or wood dowel rod ¹/₂ inch shorter

than the finished width of your shade (use tape to hold an adjustable rod at the correct length). On extra-large shades, a pulley is mounted on the heading board to house the cords and distribute the weight of the pull system.

To mount and hang the shade, you'll need a board (typically a 1 by 2) ¹/₄ inch shorter than the finished width of the shade, a staple gun, and, to attach the board to the window frame, either screws (for an inside mount or a flat mount on a door) or angle irons (for an outside mount).

For a cloud shade, buy shirring tape (see page 86).

ROLLER SHADE HARDWARE

If you're replacing an existing shade, you can simply cut new fabric to fit the roller you already have. Otherwise, you'll need to buy a roller (see page 88 for information on types of rollers and mountings). Wood rollers can be cut to size. Note the difference in the ends before you cut; the pin end is the one to cut off; the blade end contains the spring mechanism that makes the shade roll up.

With pliers, remove the pin and end cap. Cut the roller with a saw, making sure you don't cut through the spring. Replace the end cap and pound in the pin with a hammer.

The placement of your shade determines the type of brackets you'll need. One type serves an inside-mounted shade; another type is for an outside mount. Both work with either a conventional-roll or a reverse-roll shade.

A wood slat such as screen door molding, cut ¹/₂ inch shorter than the finished width of the shade, serves as a bottom stiffener and weight.

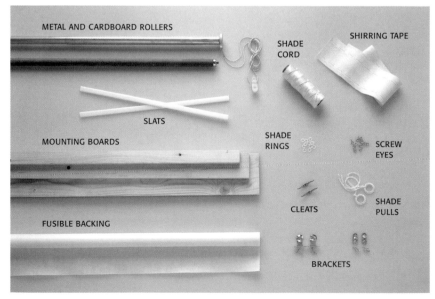

METAL AND CARDBOARD ROLLERS

SHADE CORD

SHIRRING TAPE

SLATS

MOUNTING BOARDS

SHADE RINGS

SCREW EYES

CLEATS

SHADE PULLS

FUSIBLE BACKING

BRACKETS

Typical hardware for shades includes metal rollers that must be bought to size and sturdy cardboard and wood rollers that can be cut to the necessary length.

flat roman shade

THOUGH NEARLY FLAT when unfurled, this basic Roman shade draws up into graceful, horizontal folds. This accordion effect is achieved by *pull cords* that run through columns of rings attached to the back of the shade; the vertical interval between the rings establishes the pleat depth. If you omit the dowel and place rings at the sides only, the shade will fall in one softly pleated swag instead of horizontal folds.

Because it hugs the window, a flat Roman shade insulates well. For even more protection, you can interline your shade as long as the interlining won't require seaming (the seams would show). Cut the interlining to the finished width and length, with the allowance at the top for going over the board. Slip the interlining under the pressed side and lower hems, and then treat the panel as one.

PLANNING

Decide on an inside or outside mount and note the hardware you'll need (see page 74). Typical vertical spacing between rings is 6 to 8 inches—you determine the exact vertical spacing as you make the shade. Typically, the horizontal spacing of rings is from 9 to 14 inches, depending on the width of the shade and where any seams fall. Typical skirt length is 6 inches.

If you need to join fabric widths, center a full width and add partial widths to the sides (to match pattern repeats when seaming widths, see page 26). Also, when determining where to seam your fabric, keep in mind that you should have a column of rings at each seam; you may need to adjust the horizontal spacing slightly.

CHOOSING FABRIC

Traditionally, Roman shades are lined and made in firmly woven fabrics to enable the horizontal folds to be crisp and hold their shape. But now, loosely woven fabrics, even sheers, are used to create soft-folded looks.

CALCULATING YARDAGE

Measure your window and fill in the window treatment work sheet (see pages 14–18). A Roman shade has no fullness or returns. For each seam, add a 1-inch allowance to your finished-width figure.

Finished length for an inside-mounted shade equals the length of the opening; for an outside mount, finished length is the length of the opening, plus the distance above and/or below, plus the shade's skirt.

For a patterned fabric with a repeat, plan to place a full repeat just above the bottom of the skirt.

Use the following allowances in your calculations (assuming a 6-inch skirt length):

	FABRIC	LINING
TOP	3"	3"
SIDE HEMS	3" TOTAL	1" TOTAL
SKIRT HEM	6"	5 1/2"
LOWER HEM (IF NO SKIRT)	1 1/2"	1"

FLAT ROMAN SHADE STEP-BY-STEP

1 Choose and prepare face fabric and lining, and join the fabric widths (see pages 21–26). Press seams open.

2 With face fabric wrong side up, fold up each side edge 1 1/2 inches; press. On lining, press under 1 inch on each side edge. Fold up lower skirt hem on face fabric 6 inches (if no skirt, fold up 1 1/2 inches); press. Repeat for lining, folding up 5 1/2 inches (1 inch if no skirt).

3 Lay face fabric, wrong side up, on work surface. Unfold skirt and make a small horizontal tuck in each side hem near the lower hem fold, causing side hems to widen and angle in about 1/2 inch.

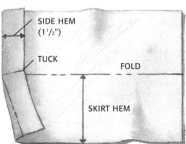

flat roman shade

4 Fold hem up again. Place lining, right side up, on face fabric so top edges are aligned and lining is ¹/₂ inch from side and lower edges. Raw edges of face fabric and lining hems should be aligned.

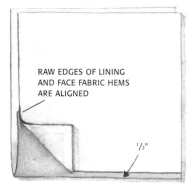

RAW EDGES OF LINING AND FACE FABRIC HEMS ARE ALIGNED

¹/₂"

5 Carefully fold back the lining to expose the raw edges of bottom hem on both layers. Without shifting layers, pin together hem edges only; then stitch 1¹/₂ inches from raw edges.

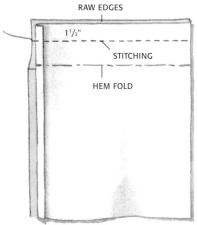

RAW EDGES

1¹/₂"

STITCHING

HEM FOLD

6 Realign lining and face fabric, wrong sides together; pin layers together along sides and across top of skirt. Stitch through all layers ¹/₄ inch below enclosed raw edges of bottom hem (you can usually see raw edges through lining), creating a 1¹/₄-inch hidden rod pocket (match top thread to lining and bobbin thread to face fabric).

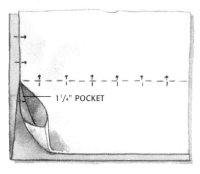

1¹/₄" POCKET

7 With layers still pinned together, the lining side up, and beginning at the top, stitch along right side ³/₄ inch from edge. Stop stitching at rod-pocket stitching. Repeat on the other side, beginning at rod-pocket stitching.

8 Place shade right side up, measure finished length from bottom of hem and mark with pins every 4 inches across width. Measure and trim top allowance to 1¹/₄ inches. Fold down top, lining side in, along pin-marked finished-length line and press. Remove pins.

9 To join lining and face fabric, serge or zigzag top edge.

10 To determine positions for columns of rings, measure width from side hem to side hem and divide by desired spacing (9 to 14 inches); round off to nearest whole number to get number of spaces. Divide width by number of spaces to arrive at exact space size. If fabric is seamed, adjust so a column of rings falls on each seam.

Place shade lining side up. At the interval determined for your space size, mark vertical lines from the rod-pocket stitching to the top. Pin lining to face fabric along marked lines, placing pins perpendicular to lines.

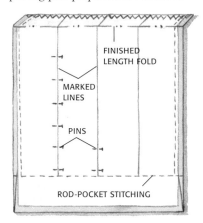

FINISHED LENGTH FOLD

MARKED LINES

PINS

ROD-POCKET STITCHING

11 Sew through all layers on each marked line.

12 The vertical space between rings (usually 6 to 8 inches) establishes the size of the pleats on the raised shade, with each pleat folding to half the space height (3 to 4 inches). To find this space, divide distance from top of pocket to the finished length fold by desired space height. Round off to nearest whole number to get number of spaces. Divide same distance by number of spaces to arrive at exact space height.

Mark ring positions at interval just determined, aligning pins horizontally.

13 Using doubled polyester thread to match lining and buttonhole stitch, sew bottom rings at rod-pocket stitching line and other rings at markings. Sew through the lining only.

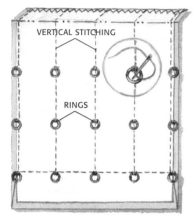

VERTICAL STITCHING

RINGS

14 Insert rod in pocket and slipstitch pocket ends closed. Also slipstitch angled folds of face fabric on each edge of hem.

15 To cover mounting board, cut a piece of fabric 1 inch wider than the distance around board and 5 inches longer on each end. Fold and staple fabric to board.

Position shade right side up over board so finished-length fold aligns with top front edge of board (for an inside or outside mount, wide face of board is up; for a flat mount on a door, wide face is against door). Staple top allowance to board.

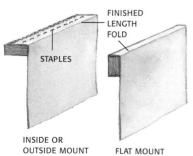

FINISHED LENGTH FOLD

STAPLES

INSIDE OR OUTSIDE MOUNT

FLAT MOUNT

16 Turn shade and board wrong side up. Insert screw eyes in bottom face of board ³/4 inch from front edge (³/8 inch on a flat-mounted shade), aligned with columns of rings.

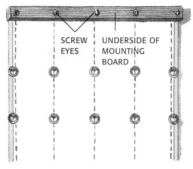

SCREW EYES

UNDERSIDE OF MOUNTING BOARD

17 For each column of rings, cut a separate length of cord long enough to go bottom ring to top ring, across top of shade to left, and halfway down side (instructions are for a shade with cords on right; to place cords on left, run cords to right).

18 With shade still wrong side up, tie one end of cord to bottom left ring and thread cord up through all rings in column; pass cord from right to left through screw eye at top and let remainder hang down left side. Repeat for each column of rings.

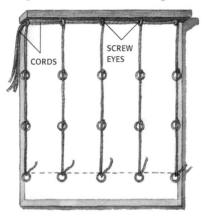

CORDS

SCREW EYES

19 Before hanging, lay shade flat, right side up; then pull cords to draw shade up to board, and secure cords with a clothespin or other clip. Straighten horizontal folds and lightly crease with your hands. When folds are arranged, tie fabric strips around board every 6 to 8 inches; keep tied for three or four days to set the folds.

20 For an inside mount, screw board directly into window frame (narrow edge faces out).

For an outside mount, measure from ceiling to position of angle iron (³/4 inch lower than top of board) on one side; also measure proper distance from side of opening. Install angle iron. Lay one end of board over angle iron. Place a carpenter's level on top of board at other end; adjust board until level. Mark position of other angle iron; install.

For a flat mount on a door, lift up shade and screw the board into the door, using a carpenter's level to check the alignment.

21 With shade unfurled, adjust tension of cords so shade draws up in even horizontal folds when cords are pulled. Lower shade and knot cords together just below right-hand screw eye.

Divide cords; braid to within 2 inches of end of shortest cord. Put cords through shade pull, knot, and trim ends. Slide pull over knot. To secure cords, mount a cleat on the window frame.

flat roman shade

swagged roman shade

A swagged Roman shade is a loose variation of a traditional Roman shade from which the bottom dowel is omitted; the shade is drawn up in only two places, forming a center swag and side tails. This style is often made in soft or semisheer fabrics and may be unlined. The effect differs slightly depending on whether you include or omit a skirt (place the bottom rings close to the lower edge to omit).

For a single window that's not overly large, sew a column of vertical rings about 6 inches in from each side to make a single swag and two tails. If the window is on the large size, you might like the effect better with wider tails. For best results, make the swag no wider 36 inches.

To use a similar treatment on a double or triple window, make one shade to cover the entire span; plan the ring settings to correspond with the window framing or mullions, creating tails at the outside edges only.

stitched roman shade

The edge of each fold on this tailored Roman shade is topstitched, creating neat horizontal tucks that are present even when the shade is lowered; the tucks act as a crisp guide for the folds when it is raised.

PLANNING

See "Flat Roman shade," page 75, for general planning guidelines. Because the pleats stack so crisply, it's better to mount this shade outside the window frame unless your window has an especially deep recess.

CHOOSING FABRIC

Fabrics that hold their shape when folded are best.

CALCULATING YARDAGE

Calculate yardage as you would for a flat Roman shade, adding in fabric for the tucks (for each tuck, allow 2 inches or twice the distance from the fold to the topstitching), as follows:

1 Determine finished length of shade; subtract skirt length.

2 The vertical space between rings (usually 6 to 8 inches) establishes the size of the pleats on the raised shade, with each pleat folding to half the space height (3 to 4 inches). To find this space, divide the result from step 1 by the desired space height; round off to nearest whole number to get number of spaces. Divide same distance by number of spaces to arrive at exact space height.

3 Multiply number of spaces by 2 inches (1 inch for each front and back tuck) and add to finished length. Add 1 inch for tuck take-up.

STITCHED ROMAN SHADE STEP-BY-STEP

1 Follow steps 1–7, "Flat Roman shade," pages 75–76, to make hems and rod pocket.

2 On back of shade, measure ½ inch from rod-pocket stitching. Pin across width every 4 inches through both layers. From pin-marked line, measure space height plus 2 inches and pin across width. Repeat up shade one less time than number of spaces.

Remaining distance should equal space height plus 1½ inches.

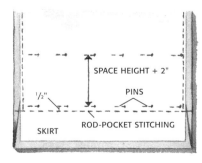

3 Turn shade right side up. Fold up on bottom row of pins. Remove pins and press fold. Repin, placing the pins perpendicular to the fold.

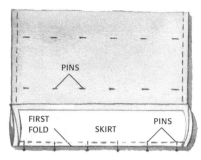

4 Make next fold on next row of pins. Repeat for all rows up back of shade.

5 Stitch parallel to each fold, ¹/₂ inch from crease, using thread to match lining; on bottom fold, stitch just to left of rod-pocket stitching.

6 Starting at bottom, bring bottom two tucks together on lining side. Crease fold on front, and pin at right angle to crease. Repeat for remaining front tucks. Stitch as for back tucks, using thread to match face fabric.

7 Follow steps 8–9, "Flat Roman shade," page 76, to measure finished length and to finish top edge.

8 Follow first part of step 10, "Flat Roman shade," page 76, to determine spacing for columns of rings across the width. Mark positions for rings on back tucks.

9 Using doubled polyester thread to match lining, sew rings through tucks on back with buttonhole stitch.

10 Follow steps 14–21, "Flat Roman shade," page 77, to finish shade.

doweled roman shade

A doweled Roman shade is constructed in the same way as a stitched Roman shade except that a rod is inserted in the front tucks only. Cut ³/₈-inch-diameter wood dowel rods, flat screen-door molding, or small PVC pipe ¹/₂ inch shorter than the finished width of the blind. To determine the tuck size, wrap scraps of fabric and lining around the rod and measure the distance between the meeting points; add some ease for the rod to move into the pocket. Adjust your yardage calculations accordingly.

After you have constructed the shade, insert the rods into the front tucks and slipstitch the ends.

---

adding a valance to a roman shade

To dress up a Roman shade, attach a valance to the mounting board. Make a band of matching or contrasting fabric with a straight or shaped lower edge, lining it if desired. Typically the length of a shade valance is about one-fifth of the total height of the shade; the width must be the same as the shade.

MAKING A SHADE VALANCE. To make the valance, include a 1¹/₂-inch top allowance, 1¹/₂ inches for the lower hem, and 3 inches total for side hems. Sew the side hems and then the bottom hem, and serge the top edge. Staple the valance to the mounting board on top of the shade.

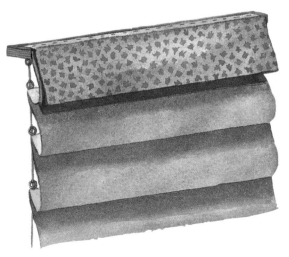

flat roman shade

soft-fold roman shade

Loops of fabric flow down the face of this shade, even when it's lowered. The face fabric is longer than the lining; it is folded to make the loops and then attached to the flat lining in a way that secures the folds whether the shade is lowered or raised.

This shade takes more time to make and requires more fabric than a flat Roman shade. The effect is equally handsome for inside and outside mounting and looks great on doors.

The distinctive horizontal lines created by the folds add a custom note to these shades. However, fabric with a pronounced motif or strong horizontal pattern may not be suitable for this treatment—test the fold interval to see how the repeat is affected.

PLANNING

Follow the planning guidelines for "Flat Roman shade," page 75, with these additional typical dimensions: The vertical spacing between rings is 5 inches, the distance between folds as seen from the front is 5 inches, each loop of fabric that becomes a soft fold requires 9 inches fabric length, and skirt length is equal to the distance between rings, plus 2 inches (7 inches in example below).

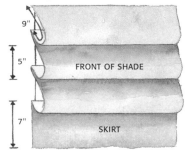

9"
5"
7"
FRONT OF SHADE
SKIRT

To determine the exact vertical space between rings, subtract the skirt length from the finished length and divide result by the desired spacing between rings; round off to the nearest whole number for the number of spaces. Divide the same distance by the number of spaces for the exact space height. Each loop will be 4 inches longer than this dimension.

The shade is raised by cords passed through columns of rings, spaced 9 to 14 inches apart depending on shade width and position of any seams.

CHOOSING FABRIC

Many fabrics suitable for flat Roman shades will also work for this shade. The fabric must be supple but not so soft that the loops flatten.

CALCULATING YARDAGE

Measure your window and fill in the window treatment work sheet (see pages 14–18). A soft-fold Roman shade has no fullness or returns. For each seam, add a 1-inch allowance to your finished-width figure.

To determine the cut length of the face fabric, one easy method is simply to double the finished length of the shade. This allows for plenty of fabric to go over the board and create the soft folds. Calculate the lining separately, adding the top allowance and skirt to the finished length. The lining is not part of the folding system and remains flat as in a flat Roman shade.

Use the following allowances in your calculations (assuming a 7-inch skirt length):

	FABRIC	LINING
TOP	3"	3"
SIDE HEMS	6" TOTAL	3" TOTAL
SKIRT HEM	7"	6½"

SOFT-FOLD ROMAN SHADE STEP-BY-STEP

1 Choose and prepare face fabric and lining, and join the fabric widths (see pages 21–26). Press the seams open.

2 With face fabric wrong side up, fold up 3 inches along each side edge; press. Turn in raw edge to meet pressed fold and press again. Repeat on lining, folding up 2 inches along each side edge.

3 On bottom edge of face fabric, fold up 7 inches for skirt hem, wrong side in; press. Repeat on the lining, folding up 6½ inches.

4 Follow steps 3–6, "Flat Roman shade," pages 75–76, to make hems and stitch rod pocket.

5 Lay shade, right side up, on work surface. From stitching at top of rod pocket, measure up 2 inches on face fabric and mark with pins across width, pinning through face fabric only.

To make the first soft fold, pinch the pin-marked line between your fingers and pull it forward and down to form a "loop" of fabric that hangs below the rod-pocket stitching.

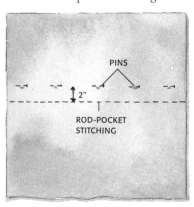

6 From pin-marked line, measure up distance to be seen between folds plus 2 inches (7 inches in example). Pin across width through face fabric and lining; place masking tape across width so lower edge of tape is on pin-marked line.

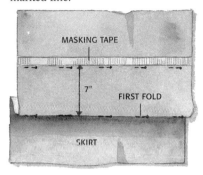

7 Measure up 2 more inches from pin-marked line on face fabric, and pin across width through face fabric only.

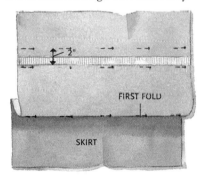

Pinch upper pin-marked line and pull it forward and down to form loop of fabric for second fold.

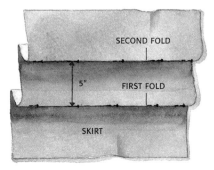

8 Repeat steps 6 and 7, ending with step 7, to form the required number of folds.

9 At second loop from bottom, lift and stitch through face fabric and lining along lower edge of tape, removing pins as you go. Repeat up face of shade. Remove tape.

10 Follow steps 8–9, "Flat Roman shade," page 76, to measure finished length and finish top edge.

11 Follow first part of step 10, "Flat Roman shade," page 76, to mark position of columns for rings (bottom rings go on the rod-pocket stitching; remaining rings go on the horizontal rows of stitching).

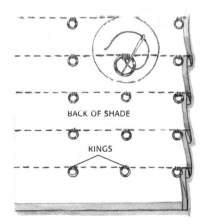

12 Using doubled polyester thread to match lining, sew rings to lining only with a buttonhole stitch.

13 Follow steps 14–18 and 20–21, "Flat Roman shade," page 77, to finish the shade.

embellishments for shades

Perhaps because the lower edge is so often at eye level, the finishing touches added to a shade make a tremendous contribution to its overall appearance. Even small details like the style of a shade pull or scale of a tassel are worth thought. And, because shades are relatively small as window treatments go, you may be able to splurge on a trimming you'd forego on something more expansive.

Tassel fringe in the same color as the shade it trims

A tiny ruffle, gathered along its middle, on a cloud shade hem

A delicate lace ruffle trimming a cloud shade hem

Jumbo cord along the top of a cloud shade, tied in a knot at the corner

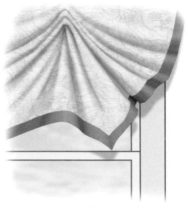

Bound edges outlining a skirted Roman shade

A coordinating skirt bordered with narrow ribbon on a Roman shade

Buttons closing the vertical pleats on a balloon or London shade

A stenciled design decorating a roller shade with a scalloped edge

A bow nestled above the pleats on a tailed cloud shade

balloon shade

TRUE TO ITS NAME, a balloon shade is airy and rounded, with deep inverted pleats that fall into poufs at the bottom. You draw the shade up using cords threaded through rings. On some balloon shades, the bottom pouf remains when the shade is completely lowered, an effect that is achieved by adding to the length and tying the lower rings together.

PLANNING
These directions are for an outside-mounted balloon shade. Note the hardware and notions you'll need (see page 74).

On a balloon shade, each fabric width will make a half-pleat, a space, a full pleat, a space, and another half-pleat (size depends on board size and usable fabric widths).

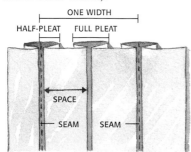

For unpatterned fabric or fabric with an allover pattern, first try a space size of 10 inches. If your fabric has large motifs, analyze the design and choose space and pleat sizes that will place the same part of the motif in each space.

You'll add returns to cover the ends of the board once you've seamed the widths. A half-pleat extends to each end of the face board; the return and side hem are beyond.

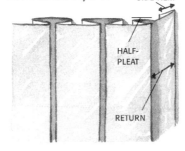

Vertical spacing of rings can range from 6 to 10 inches, depending on depth desired for horizontal folds.

CHOOSING FABRIC
Select a fabric that's firm enough to hold pleats and soft enough to form poufs.

CALCULATING YARDAGE
Follow these steps to arrive at pleat and space sizes and yards needed. In the following example, the board is $1\frac{1}{2}$ inches wide by 48 inches long and the fabric is 54 inches wide.

1 Measure your window and fill in the window treatment work sheet (pages 14–18) to arrive at board size. Return size is equal to depth of board.

2 Divide board size by 10 inches (trial space size); round off to nearest whole number for number of spaces ($48 \div 10 = 4.8$; rounds to 5). Divide board size by number of spaces for exact space size ($48 \div 5 = 9.6$ or $9\frac{5}{8}$ inches).

3 Subtract exact space size from half the usable fabric width (26 inches for fabric with 52 inches usable fabric) for pleat loop size ($26 - 9\frac{5}{8} = 16\frac{3}{8}$ inches). When flattened, each full pleat will be half the loop size (about $8\frac{1}{8}$ inches).

4 To determine number of fabric widths needed, divide number of spaces (from step 2) by 2. If result is a whole number, add a width; if result contains a half-width, round up to next whole number. Continue to fill in second row of work sheet.

Also use the following allowances in your calculations:

	FABRIC	LINING
TOP	3"	3"
LOWER HEM		
with pouf	21"	18"
without pouf	3"	NONE

BALLOON SHADE STEP-BY-STEP

1 Choose and prepare face fabric and lining (see pages 21–26).

2 *If you have an odd number of spaces,* join fabric widths as described on page 26; press seams open. Lay face fabric right side up; measure, mark, and trim a quarter-width from the width at far right. Pin and stitch this piece to the width at far left.

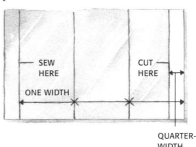

balloon shade

Press seam open. From this seam, measure and mark a distance equal to return plus 1½ inches; trim excess. From right seam, measure a distance equal to a half-width; from this point, measure and mark a distance equal to return plus 1½ inches; trim. Repeat on lining so seams will align with those on face fabric; trim 1 inch on each side.

If you have an even number of spaces, join all widths except one. Split this width and sew half to one side and half to other side; press seams open. From each end seam, measure and mark toward edge a distance equal to return plus 1½ inches; cut fabric. Repeat on lining so seams will align with those on face fabric; trim 1 inch on each side.

3 Place face fabric wrong side up. Fold up each side edge 1½ inches; press. Repeat on lining, folding up each side edge 1 inch.

4 Lay face fabric wrong side up. Place lining, right side up, on face fabric ½ inch in from side edges; lower edge of lining should be 3 inches above lower edge of face fabric. Pin at side edges and stitch through all layers ¾ inch from edge of face fabric; continue stitching to lower edge of face fabric (match top thread to lining and bobbin thread to face fabric).

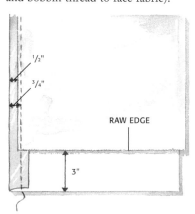

5 With lining still turned right side up, measure and mark vertical guidelines for stitching at midpoint of each full width. For a shade with an odd number of spaces, also measure and mark a line where return begins on unseamed side edge. Pin all seams and marked lines. Beginning at raw edge of lining at lower hem, stitch on marked lines and seams.

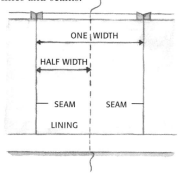

6 Turn shade right side up and, on right edge, measure from line of return stitching toward center a distance equal to a half-pleat loop; pin vertically down length of shade.

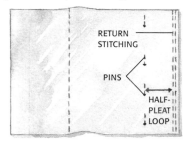

To form half-pleat, bring pin-marked line to return stitching. Pin together close to front and back folds. Repeat on other edge.

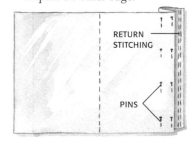

7 Measure and mark same distance on either side of each row of vertical stitching. To form a full pleat, bring each pin-marked line to row of stitching; pin in place vertically near front folds so pleats "kiss." Space size must be as determined earlier; adjust pleats if necessary.

Pin through all layers where pleats form folds on back.

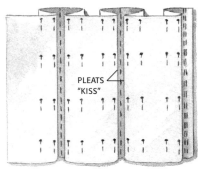

8 Turn shade lining side up. To hold pleats in place, edgestitch all folds from raw edge of lining to lower edge of face fabric, backstitching at beginning and end.

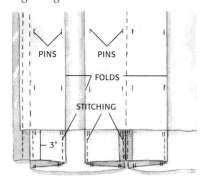

9 At bottom edge, turn up face fabric 3 inches; press. Turn raw edge in to meet pressed fold and press again. Stitch lower hem close to second fold to form rod pocket.

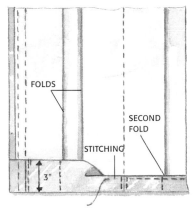

10 Turn shade right side up. On one edge, fold back return along return stitching. Then, fold edge of shade forward to meet return stitching, forming a ³/₄-inch pleat. On the wrong side, hand-stitch pleat to lower edge of pocket.

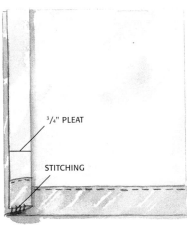

11 On right side of shade, measure finished length from bottom of hem and mark with pins every 4 inches across width. Measure and trim top allowances ¹/₄ inch narrower than board. Fold down top allowance, lining side in, along pin-marked finished-length line; press. Remove the pins. Press the pleats in place above the finished-length line.

To join face fabric and lining, serge or zigzag top edge.

12 With pins, mark each ring position, aligning rings horizontally (the rings will be sewn to side hem stitching and vertical stitching, but not return stitching). Place the bottom rings at the top of the rod pocket and the other rings 6 to 10 inches apart.

13 Follow step 13, "Flat Roman shade," page 77, to sew on rings, being careful not to catch side edges of pleats.

14 Cover one end of the rod with masking tape and insert in pocket; slipstitch closed. Form a ³/₄-inch pleat, same as on other end; hand-stitch the pleat to lower edge of pocket.

15 Follow steps 15–18 and 20–21, "Flat Roman shade," page 77, with these changes or additions: In step 15, fold and staple return portion of top allowance to each board end; in step 18, tie together lower four rings in each column to create a permanent pouf at lower edge; and in step 21, disregard reference to folds.

london shade

A London shade is a cousin to the swagged Roman shade in looks, but it is made like a balloon shade, with just two inverted pleats widely spaced and the side rigging and bottom dowel omitted. The soft scallop and tails are formed when the two bottom rows of rigging rings are tied together. As the shade is raised, the scalloping and draping increase, creating an even softer look.

cloud shade

SOFT SHIRRING across the top differentiates the cloud shade from the balloon shade. The tape used to achieve this look comes in a variety of patterns, from simple gathers to pencil pleats and smocking. The poufed, gently scalloped draping is accomplished by pulling cords that run through columns of rings attached to the back of the shade.

PLANNING

These directions are for an outside-mounted cloud shade. Note the hardware and notions you'll need (see page 74). Buy shirring tape equal in length to total shade width. Two-cord tape, the narrowest, creates about an inch of shirring; four-cord tape creates about 4 inches.

For the heading (the ruffle above the shirring), choose a height according to the width of the tape. With two-cord tape, a 2- to 3-inch tall heading is appropriate. With three- or four-cord tape, the heading is usually ½ inch.

Vertical spacing of the rings can range from 6 to 10 inches, depending on depth desired for horizontal folds.

To create a base for the rings on an unlined sheer shade, sew ¼-inch vertical tucks midway between seams joining widths. Press the tucks to one side and stitch them to the face fabric. Sew the rings to the tucks, keeping vertical spacing equal.

CHOOSING FABRIC

A cloud shade made from a crisp fabric will hold its shape and provide good light control and privacy. One made from batiste, gauze, or lace will hang in soft folds and filter light.

CALCULATING YARDAGE

The following project assumes a 1½-inch-wide mounting board.

1 Measure your window and fill in window treatment work sheet (see pages 14–18) to arrive at board size. Add 3 inches for two 1½-inch returns. (If, for example, your board is 60 inches long, adjusted board size would be 63 inches.)

2 Divide adjusted board size by 10 inches (trial space size); round off to the nearest whole number for the number of spaces (63 ÷ 10 = 6.3; rounds to 6).

3 To determine number of widths, divide number of spaces by 2 (each width of fabric will make two spaces, or scallops); if result contains a half-width, round up to next whole number.

Continue to fill in second row of work sheet, using number of widths just determined. Use following allowances in your calculations:

	FABRIC	LINING
TOP	HEADING SIZE + ½"	NONE
LOWER HEMS	21"	18"

CLOUD SHADE STEP-BY-STEP

1 Choose and prepare face fabric and lining; join the fabric widths (see pages 21–26) so the seams on face fabric and lining will align. Press seams open.

2 For an odd number of spaces, measure and cut a half-width from right or left width on face fabric. Trim lining 1 inch narrower than face fabric on each side.

3 Follow steps 3–4, "Balloon shade," page 84, to join lining and face fabric and to make side hems.

4 With lining right side up, measure and mark vertical guidelines for stitching at midpoint of each full width. Pin marked lines and seams. Beginning at raw edge of lining at lower hem, stitch on marked lines and seams.

5 At bottom edge, turn up face fabric 3 inches; press. Turn raw edge in to meet pressed fold and press again. Stitch lower hem close to second fold to form rod pocket.

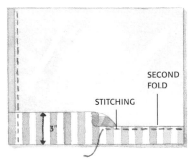

6 Follow step 12, "Balloon shade," page 85, to mark ring positions (disregard reference to return stitching).

7 On right side of shade, measure finished length from bottom of hem and mark with pins every 4 inches across width. Measure proper top allowance beyond finished-length line; trim. Remove stitching at top of each side hem to finished-length line. Place shade lining side up and trim lining so the upper edge meets the pin-marked line.

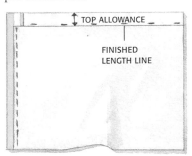

8 With lining still on top, fold down top allowance, wrong side in, on finished-length line; press. Remove pins. Position shirring tape, right side up, on back of shade, turning under ends and placing top edge 3/4 inch above raw edge.

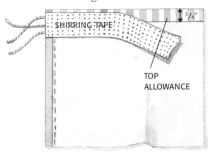

Pin, stitch, and gather tape following steps 3–5 for "Pencil pleats" on page 67 (tape should be gathered to the adjusted board size).

9 Follow step 13, "Flat Roman shade," page 77, to sew on rings.

10 Follow first part of step 15, "Flat Roman shade," page 77, to cover mounting board.

11 Staple shade to face and ends of mounting board, placing staples vertically 2 inches apart and concealing them between gathers. Insert dowel in pocket and slipstitch closed; adjust fullness and staple pocket to dowel every 6–8 inches.

12 Follow steps 16–18, "Flat Roman shade," page 77. In step 18, tie together lower four rings in each row to create pouf.

13 Follow steps 20–21, "Flat Roman shade," page 77, to finish shade (disregard reference to folds in step 21).

ruffled cloud shade

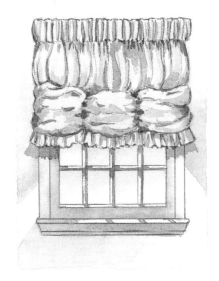

A ruffled bottom adds a frilly finish to a cloud shade. You'll need extra fabric for the ruffle. Trim hem allowance to 1/2 inch on face fabric and lining. Fold and press side hems on face fabric and lining. See pages 42–43 to make a folded ruffle and attach it to the lower edge of face fabric.

Center lining over face fabric and ruffle and sew over previous stitches.

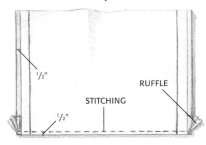

Turn face fabric and lining right side out and lightly press. With lining side up, pin side edges together. Starting at upper right and using 3/4-inch seam allowance, stitch down side edge, across bottom, and up other side, pivoting at corners. Follow steps 7–13, "Cloud shade," at left, to finish.

roller shade

OF ALL THE shade styles, the roller shade requires the least amount of fabric and work—there are no seams, side hems, folds, or gathers. And, because the shade is flat, the fabric's pattern shows clearly. Add a valance or cornice to hide the roller handsomely.

Two cautions: The width of a roller shade can't exceed the usable width of your fabric—seams are very obvious and won't roll up smoothly. Also, roller shades are not recommended for windows more than 5 feet tall.

PLANNING AND INSTALLATION

Because you won't know the thickness of the shade until it's finished, make the shade before installing the brackets. When you install them, be sure to position them so the roller will be perfectly level.

For a conventional-roll shade, where the fabric unrolls to the back, the blade end of the roller should be on your left as you face the window. Mount the slotted bracket on the left side. *For a reverse-roll shade,* where the fabric unrolls to the front, mount the slotted bracket on the right side.

CHOOSING FABRIC AND BACKING

Look for a firmly woven all-cotton or other natural-fiber fabric that won't fray easily. Avoid fabrics with heavy finishes, which may prevent the backing from adhering to the fabric.

If selecting a blend that contains synthetic fibers, test samples of fabric and backing to make sure the fabric bonds well before purchasing the entire amount of fabric.

Fusible shade backing, a heat-sensitive material made especially for shades, stiffens the fabric and, if it is a blackout backing, blocks light. Backings come in varying widths; look for them in fabric stores.

CALCULATING YARDAGE

The finished width of your shade is equal to the desired length of the roller. The piece of fabric must be 3 inches wider than the finished shade width and 12 inches longer than the finished length (for wrapping around the roller). Buy enough fabric to place a full pattern repeat just above the slat and to center a repeat horizontally. Purchase a piece of fusible backing the same size as the fabric.

ROLLER SHADE STEP-BY-STEP

1 Choose and prepare face fabric (see pages 21–26).

2 Square off one end of face fabric. Measure total length of shade; square and cut other end.

3 Fuse the shade fabric and backing, following the manufacturer's instructions and working from center to sides and from top to bottom.

4 Measure and mark side edges to finished width, keeping lines straight and corners square. Cut along lines with a rotary cutter or sharp scissors, making long, clean strokes and keeping fabric perfectly flat.

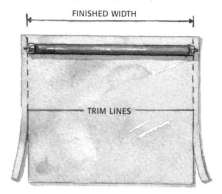

5 With backing side up, turn up lower edge 1½ inches; finger-press fold. Stitch 1¼ inches from edge, using longest straight-stitch setting. Insert a wood slat in pocket.

6 Align top edge of shade with guideline on roller (if roller has no guideline, hold roller firmly on a table and, with marker lying flat on table, draw a line along roller.)

7 Attach shade to roller with masking tape, aligning edge with guideline; be sure orientation is correct for your chosen direction of roll. To check that shade is straight, roll by hand and insert in brackets. If shade is crooked, unroll and adjust. If roller is wood, staple shade to roller using ¼-inch staples; pound in staples with a hammer if necessary.

8 To prevent fraying, put a small amount of liquid fray preventer on your finger and draw it along the edge; let dry completely before raising shade.

great roller shade hem shapes

Roller shades may begin as plain rectangles enlivened only by their fabric, but changes to the shape of their hemlines add the elegance and punch that make them a good fit for diverse decorating styles. Use a facing to finish the hem (page 101).

Alternating large points and scallops, with a center point

Three large scallops, with the center one lower than those on the sides

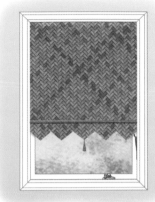

A large zigzag edge

A delicate scalloped edge

Quirky, unequal zigzags

A bold scalloped edge

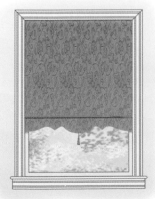

Alternating large points and scallops, with a center scallop

Alternating small points and scallops, with a center scallop

valances

BELOW TOP: Valances with a bold zigzag hemline turn extra playful with stripes placed sideways over their Roman shade mates.

BELOW BOTTOM: A simple straight valance becomes a bit of a flirt when it's mounted flat across the middle but gathered at each end.

RIGHT: For romance, place a rod-pocket valance with a gently arched hemline between matching curtains tied high up— use three curtains and two valances on closely spaced windows like these.

RIGHT: *If you're looking for a jaunty window topper, go for a rolled stagecoach valance with a contrast lining and ties. This one is mounted over a roller shade with a tab-supported rod at the hemline.*

BELOW: *An easier alternative to a formal cornice, this flat valance features a dramatically shaped hemline, tassel fringe, and large tassels. It is inside-mounted.*

OPPOSITE: *These valances start as flat rectangles with fringe at the hem; their side edges are permanently pleated to give a swag effect. To get this look, make a mockup in muslin first to work out the pleat configuration. You could bind the edges after pleating or tack the pleats together by hand.*

valances

RIGHT: *To make a pinch-pleat valance like this one, shown over a matching fringed, skirted Roman shade, adapt the directions for pinch-pleat draperies; then staple to the front edge of the mounting board.*

BELOW: *This tasseled valance with a zigzag hemline is shirred vertically between the points. Pull up two cords on shirring tape to get this effect.*

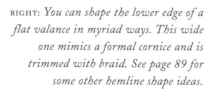

RIGHT: *You can shape the lower edge of a flat valance in myriad ways. This wide one mimics a formal cornice and is trimmed with braid. See page 89 for some other hemline shape ideas.*

Contrast borders add snappy definition to top and side treatments made from the same fabric; they also take attention away from the fact that the fabric pattern may not match from top to bottom. The pleats on this valance are symmetrical but spaced with a larger flat area in the middle—an attractive option on a double window.

how to make valances

WHETHER USED ALONE or with other treatments, fabric valances soften and frame windows. Some types, such as rod-pocket and balloon valances, can be thought of simply as shortened curtains or shades; other valances are unique. Shaped valances add a graceful inner curve to the window while straight valances finish off the top edge. A valance used over another treatment helps conceal the hardware.

Though styles may be different, most valances call for a lining attached at the lower hem. Sewing the lining in with the face fabric at the lower edge ensures a neat, professional look.

fabric needs

Often you'll use the same fabric for the valance as for the undertreatment. Where there's no undertreatment, or if the valance is made from a contrasting fabric, choose the same sort of fabric you would for a full-length version. Also take a look at the individual project for specific recommendations.

length guidelines

Most valances begin 8 inches above the window opening, though this can vary depending on what's underneath. Finished length for straight valances is from 12 to 18 inches; shaped valances can be considerably longer on the sides, sometimes reaching to the sill.

Long valances can reduce light, interfere with the view, and visually shorten windows. If you like the look of a deep valance, consider starting it farther above the window opening.

hardware

Rod-pocket and related shaped valances hang from curtain rods (see at left and pages 38–39); install the rod as described on page 39. The rod can be mounted on the inside or outside of the window frame, depending on the look you want. Other valances, such as pleated and balloon styles, are board-mounted. A valance used alone requires a board at least $1^{1}/_{2}$ inches deep; one used over other treatments requires a board deep enough to clear whatever is underneath and to cover the hardware used for the undertreatment.

WOOD ROD WITH INSIDE MOUNT

DECORATIVE RODS

CAFÉ RODS

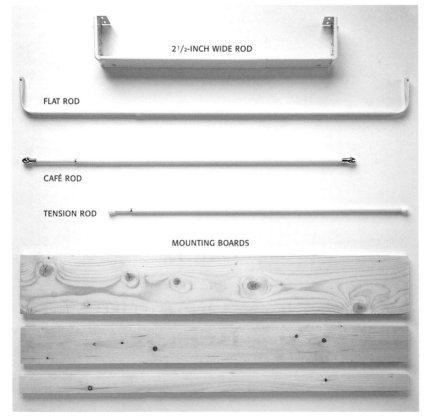

$2^{1}/_{2}$-INCH WIDE ROD

FLAT ROD

CAFÉ ROD

TENSION ROD

MOUNTING BOARDS

LEFT: *Hardware for valances includes decorative curtain and drapery rods, basic curtain rods, and mounting boards, each appropriate for different styles of valances.*

rod-pocket valance

THIS BASIC VALANCE style looks just like a short rod-pocket curtain, but the order of fabrication is different, and the lining hem fold does not float loosely over the face fabric hem.

CALCULATING YARDAGE

Measure your window and fill in the window treatment work sheet (see pages 14–18). For most fabrics, a fullness of 3 times the finished width is best. For length guidelines, see page 96.

Use the following allowances in your calculations. Refer to the top chart on page 53 for pocket size.

	FABRIC	LINING
LOWER HEMS	3"	1½"
SIDE HEMS	5" TOTAL	NONE
TOP	2 × POCKET + 2 × HEADING (IF USED)	NONE

ROD-POCKET VALANCE STEP-BY-STEP

1 Choose and prepare face fabric and lining, joining fabric widths as described (see pages 21–26). Press seams open.

2 With right sides together, pin and stitch face fabric to lining at lower edge, centering lining on face fabric and using a 1½-inch seam allowance. Press seam allowances toward face fabric. Fold and press lower hem so 1½ inches of face fabric shows on lining side of valance.

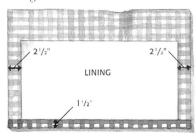

3 On right side of face fabric, measure from lower edge a distance equal to finished length and mark with pins every 4 inches across valance. Measure and mark proper top allowance (2 times pocket plus 2 times heading, if desired) above pin-marked finished-length line. Trim ravel allowance. Trim lining so upper edge meets pin-marked finished-length line.

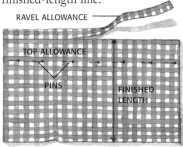

4 Turn valance wrong side up. For side hems, turn face fabric 2½ inches to the wrong side and press. Turn raw edge in to meet pressed fold and press again. Fold corners diagonally to form miter. Blindhem by machine or hand-slipstitch hem to lining only.

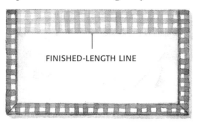

5 Fold top edge of fabric toward lining along finished-length line; press. Remove pins. Turn raw edge in to meet the pressed fold and press again. Stitch close to the second fold. For heading, if used, stitch again from the top fold a distance equal to the heading depth; press.

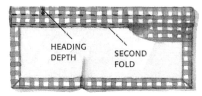

6 Slip rod through pocket between back two layers of fabric, gathering fabric evenly.

pouf valance

Sometimes called a mock balloon, a pouf valance has a rod pocket at the top and the hanging portion is double-layered to allow the fabric to spread apart into crisp peaks and poufs.

CALCULATING YARDAGE

Measure your window and fill in the window treatment work sheet (see pages 14–18). For most fabrics, a fullness of 3 times the finished width is best.

To determine finished length, make a sketch of your window. Finished length is equal to the distance covered above the window opening, plus the amount that extends into the opening times 2.

Typically, a valance used alone or over an inside-mounted treatment starts 8 inches above the opening, extends 4 inches into the opening and doubles back on itself completely. (Finished length in example is 24 inches.)

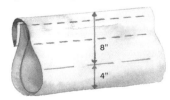

A valance over draperies might start 15 inches above the opening (near or at the ceiling) and extend 3 inches into the opening.

Use the following allowances in your calculations. Refer to the top chart on page 53 for pocket size.

	FABRIC	LINING
LOWER HEMS	POCKET + HEADING	POCKET + HEADING
SIDE HEMS	5" TOTAL	NONE
TOP	2 × POCKET + 2 × HEADING (IF USED)	2 × POCKET + 2 × HEADING (IF USED)

POUF VALANCE STEP-BY-STEP

1 Choose and prepare face fabric and lining, and join the fabric widths (see pages 21–26). Press seams open. On right side of face fabric, measure from lower edge a distance equal to finished length. Mark with pins every 4 inches across valance.

2 Center lining on face fabric, wrong sides together, aligning top and bottom raw edges. For side hems, turn face fabric 2½ inches to the wrong side and press. Turn raw edge in to meet pressed fold and press again. Blindhem by machine or hand-slipstitch hem to lining only.

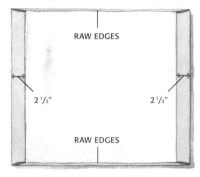

RAW EDGES

2½"   2½"

RAW EDGES

3 Measure and mark top allowance (2 times pocket plus 2 times heading, if used) above pin-marked finished-length line. Trim ravel allowance.

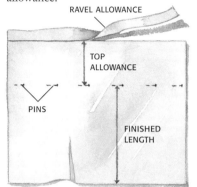

RAVEL ALLOWANCE

TOP ALLOWANCE

PINS

FINISHED LENGTH

4 Fold top allowance to wrong side along pin-marked finished-length line; press. Fold raw edge in to meet pressed fold and press again. Remove pins. Fold entire piece, lining side in, tucking in bottom raw edge until it meets first fold. Stitch close to second fold. For heading, if used, stitch again from top fold a distance equal to heading depth; press.

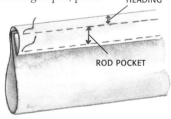

HEADING

ROD POCKET

5 Slip rod through pocket between back two layers of fabric, gathering fabric evenly. Pull layers apart to create pouf. Add crumpled tissue paper, if you like, to help keep the pouf shape.

arched valance

This gathered valance forms a graceful curve along its lower edge. The arch should be gentle; a sharply arched valance, when gathered, won't curve evenly along its lower edge and the lining may be visible from the front.

CALCULATING YARDAGE

Measure your window and fill in the window treatment work sheet (see pages 14–18). For most fabrics, a fullness of 3 times the finished width is best. Finished length is the longest point at the sides.

For the most pleasing appearance, the difference between the long and short points of the arch should be no more than 8 inches and no less than 3 inches. A typical finished side length is 18 inches, with a finished center length of 10 inches.

Use the following allowances in your calculations. Refer to the top chart on page 53 for pocket size. If you plan to add a ruffle, piping, or facing, buy extra fabric.

	FABRIC	LINING
LOWER HEMS	½"	½"
SIDE HEMS	5" TOTAL	NONE
TOP	2 × POCKET + 2 × HEADING (IF USED)	2 × POCKET + 2 × HEADING (IF USED)

ARCHED VALANCE STEP-BY-STEP

1 Choose and prepare face fabric and lining, joining fabric widths as described (see pages 21–26). Press seams open.

2 With wrong sides together, center and pin lining to face fabric, aligning top and bottom raw edges.

3 On right side of face fabric, measure top allowance (2 times pocket plus 2 times heading, if used) above pin-marked finished-length line. Mark with pins across valance.

4 Draw a rectangular paper pattern ½ inch longer than finished length and half the finished width of valance. Divide vertically into fourths.

For valance center, measure and mark the shortest point plus ½ inch for hem allowance (10½ inches in example) from the top edge on one end. Draw a line at depth of return parallel to opposite end. For side of valance, mark longest point plus ½ inch (18½ inches in example) on return line. Subtract short distance from long and divide by 4 to find increment for curve (2 inches).

Add the curve increment to the dimension marked on center line. On next vertical line, mark the distance equal to this sum below top edge with a standing pin. Continue adding the increment to the previous distance and pinning at vertical lines. Then move the three pins up to strike a gentle arc, moving the middle pin up most. Mark the curve.

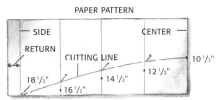

5 Cut out pattern and lay on half of valance, placing top edge of pattern on finished-length line; mark curved cutting line. Flip pattern and mark other half of valance. Cut face fabric and lining on line. Remove pins.

6 *For a same-fabric facing* (see page 101), stitch facing to lower edge of lining. *For trim* (see page 101), apply to lower edge of face fabric.

7 Pin the lower edges of face fabric and lining right sides together. Stitch, using ½-inch seam allowance; trim and clip the seam allowances. Turn right side out and press the lower edge. Trim lining so upper edge meets pin-marked finished-length line.

8 For side hems, turn face fabric 2½ inches to the wrong side and press. Turn raw edge in to meet pressed fold and press again. Blindhem by machine or hand-slipstitch hem to lining only.

9 Follow steps 5–6, "Rod-pocket valance," page 97, to finish valance.

tapered valance

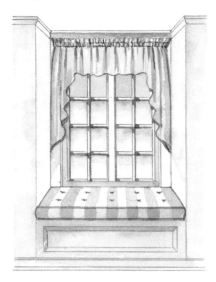

This easy-to-make, gathered valance cascades down the sides of a window, framing the view. It uses a minimum of fabric. A contrast lining looks nice, especially on a longer valance.

When calculating the yardage, allow a full width for each tapered side panel and another full width (or more for especially wide windows) for the center portion. Fullness is 3 times the finished width.

Make the center panel 12 to 18 inches long. Tapered valances look best when the side panels are either one-third or two-thirds longer than the center panel.

Use the same calculations as "Arched valance," page 99, and follow steps 1–3. Refer to step 4 to make a paper pattern. On the center line, measure and mark finished length at center plus ½ inch for hem allowance.

Repeat for inner corner where center and side widths meet. Draw a line connecting the two points. Draw a line at depth of return parallel to opposite end. On return line, measure and mark outer finished length plus ½ inch. Draw a line from inner corner to bottom of return, rounding corners, for the lower edge of the valance.

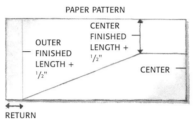

To complete the valance, follow steps 5–9, "Arched valance," page 99.

scalloped valance

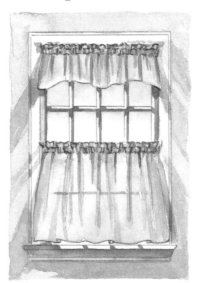

A gently undulating lower hem sets this valance style apart from other shaped valances.

For most fabrics, a fullness of 3 times the finished width is best. The finished length is based on the longest points at the sides. For a scalloped valance over traversing draperies or stationary side panels, the sides and center are often the same length. For a valance over blinds, a shade, or café curtains, the sides are often longer.

Make the shortest portions of the valance anywhere from 12 to 18 inches long and then make the longest portions 5 inches longer.

Use the same allowances and follow the same basic instructions as for an "Arched valance," page 99, with the following adjustments to the paper pattern:

For a valance with sides and center at same length, mark shortest length plus ½ inch at third (middle) vertical line; draw a horizontal line through this point across pattern. Add another horizontal line midway between this line and the bottom edge. Draw a gentle arc that passes through the intersection of each horizontal and vertical line. Cut out pattern.

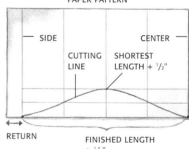

finishing shaped valances

SOMETIMES, the lower edges of arched, tapered, and scalloped valances may reveal a bit of the lining from the front. If you wish to hide or disguise the lining, you have several options.

One easy solution is to line the valance with a complementary fabric. Or you can add a ruffle or narrow piping to the lower edge. Still another approach is to stitch a same-fabric facing to the lower edge of the lining. You can also topstitch a contrast band to the shaped edge.

Whichever finish you choose, complete your valance following steps 7–9 for "Arched valance" on page 99.

ruffles

To make a ruffle, refer to "Adding decorative edgings," pages 42–43.

1 With raw edges aligned, pin ruffle to lower edge of face fabric, aligning ends of ruffle with side hem folds.

2 Baste, using ¹/₂-inch seam allowance.

flat piping

For ¹/₂-inch flat piping, you'll need a 2-inch-wide strip of bias-cut contrast fabric equal in length to the edge to be trimmed plus 1 inch. For ¹/₄-inch piping, make the strip 1¹/₂ inches wide. (Bias-cut strips work best on curved edges but require more fabric.) Note that the piping may not hide the lining.

1 Fold strip in half lengthwise, wrong side in; press. At one end, open strip and turn in ¹/₂ inch; finger-press.

2 With raw edges aligned, pin piping to lower edge of face fabric, aligning folded end of strip with side hem fold on valance. Using ¹/₂-inch seam allowance, baste together; turn in other end of piping to align with opposite hem fold.

same-fabric facing

Add 3 inches plus the difference between the longest and shortest points on valance to the cut length on your work sheet. Subtract ¹/₂ inch from amount just figured; subtract the result from the lining length.

1 Cut valance and facing from face fabric. Cut lining as a rectangle.

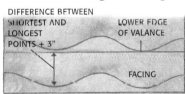
DIFFERENCE BETWEEN SHORTEST AND LONGEST POINTS + 3"   LOWER EDGE OF VALANCE   FACING

2 With right sides together and using ¹/₂-inch seam allowance, sew straight edge of facing to bottom of lining.

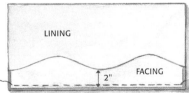
LINING   FACING   2"

3 Press the facing away from the lining and the seam toward it.

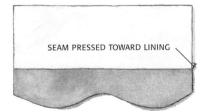
SEAM PRESSED TOWARD LINING

contrast band

You'll need two strips of fabric, each as long as the total valance width. The width of the strips should equal the distance between the high and low points on the lower edge, plus the desired finished width of the band (typically 1 to 2 inches), plus 1 inch for two seam allowances.

1 Lay strips right sides together, aligning raw edges. Place pattern on top, aligning curve on lower edge; draw shape on strip. Move pattern up a distance equal to finished width of band plus 1 inch. Mark upper curve. Cut on marked lines.

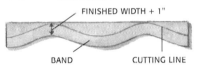
FINISHED WIDTH + 1"   BAND   CUTTING LINE

2 Pin and stitch strips together on top edge using ¹/₂-inch seam allowance. Trim seam allowance. Turn right side out; press edge.

3 Place band on right side of valance, aligning unfinished edges; baste together. Topstitch finished edge of band to valance. After valance is lined, topstitch through all layers along lower edge of band.

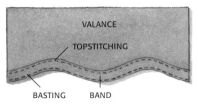
VALANCE   TOPSTITCHING   BASTING   BAND

tab stagecoach valance

This jaunty valance, made in much the same way as a rod-pocket curtain, is inside-mounted on a tension rod. Two simple loop tabs hold the valance up at the ends, forming a slightly curved lower edge and tails. The tension rod mounting is best used for a narrow window.

The valance fabric is doubled to form a self-lining, which prevents the wrong side from showing when the lower edge is folded up on itself.

CHOOSING FABRIC

Select a firmly woven fabric that will hold its shape, such as sailcloth or duck. Patterned fabric may show through when doubled; to test, hold two layers of the fabric up to the light to see the effect.

A striped fabric is ideal because the stripes line up and won't show through when the fabric is doubled. With a striped fabric, consider running the stripes vertically on the valance and horizontally on the tabs.

CALCULATING YARDAGE

Total width equals the width of the window opening, less $^1/_4$ inch, plus 1 inch for two $^1/_2$-inch side hems, plus 2 inches for ease pleats. Cut length is equal to 2 times the finished length (12 to 14 inches is a good range for finished length), plus 2 times the pocket size (see the top chart on page 53), plus a 1-inch ravel allowance.

For tabs, you'll need two strips of fabric, each twice the desired finished width ($1^1/_2$ to 2 inches, depending on the width of the valance), plus 1 inch for two $^1/_2$-inch seam allowances. The cut length of each strip is 2 times the finished length.

TAB STAGECOACH VALANCE STEP-BY-STEP

1 Choose and prepare fabric (see pages 21–26).

2 On right side of fabric, measure from lower edge a distance equal to 2 times finished length and mark with pins every 4 inches across valance width. Then measure and mark 2 times pocket size above finished-length line. Trim ravel allowance.

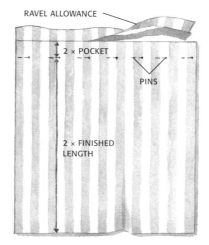

RAVEL ALLOWANCE

2 × POCKET

PINS

2 × FINISHED LENGTH

3 Fold panel, right side in, so lower raw edge is on pin-marked finished-length line.

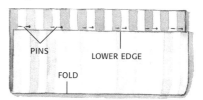

PINS

LOWER EDGE

FOLD

4 Pin and stitch layers together on each side edge, using $^1/_2$-inch seam allowance. Trim allowance at corners.

5 Turn right side out and press edges. Fold down top edge, wrong side in, on finished-length line; press. Turn raw edge in to meet pressed fold and press again. Stitch close to second fold.

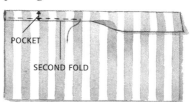

POCKET

SECOND FOLD

6 For tabs, cut two strips to desired dimensions. Fold each strip in half lengthwise, right side in, and pin. Stitch, using $^1/_2$-inch seam allowance. Turn right side out. Press, centering seam at back. Overlap ends and pin.

7 Slip rod through pocket of valance. Pinch 1-inch-deep pleats at the points where the tabs will be placed and slipstitch. This prevents the tails from swinging into the window too far.

8 Fold up valance, and slip tabs over pleats to check length. Adjust tab length to your liking; repin. Remove tabs; slipstitch the ends. Replace tabs on valance, positioning the stitched ends on the back near the top so they do not show. Place rod in window.

rolled stagecoach valance

This self-lined valance is rolled up and tied in the center. It can be stapled to a 1½-inch board for an inside or outside mount or used on a tension rod for an inside mount. Use this valance only on a narrow window.

Yardage calculations are similar to the tab stagecoach valance, except that you allow extra length for the roll. Before you buy the fabric, unroll and fold the fabric 20 inches over itself; roll up. Experiment until you arrive at a pleasing roll; then measure the fabric and add to the visible length to arrive at the finished length.

Fabric ties or ribbons can be used as the carrier, which usually looks best if the bow is made separately and applied after the carrier is in place. The carrier should be stapled to the top of a mounting board, or sewn into the rod pocket and wrapped under the roll and then up and around to the back of the tension rod.

shade-style valances

These stationary valances are shortened versions of Roman, balloon, and cloud shades. To make them, refer to the instructions for "Swagged Roman shade," page 78, "Balloon shade," page 83, and "Cloud shade," page 86.

Typically, shade-style valances are from 20 to 25 inches long before they are raised. If rings are sewn to the back, the cords are adjusted for proper tension and tied to each screw eye. Many times, it is not necessary to sew on rings. Instead, simply whipstitch the folds together where rings would have been placed and eliminate the cords.

When making a cloud valance, you may substitute a rod pocket for the shirring tape at the top edge and gather the fabric on a rod. Omit the side rings to create tails.

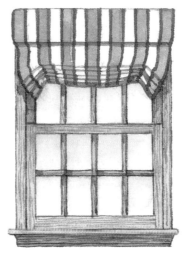

A tailed Roman valance with a matching valance of its own

A balloon valance with four poufed sections (three pleats)

A cloud valance rigged to fall in four poufed sections

embellishments for valances

A thoughtfully chosen accent makes a valance look custom-designed and truly finished. Accents needn't be showy or extravagant to be effective—a well-placed, well-proportioned bow or a subtle tassel may add just the perfect touch.

Woven braid topstitched above a curved lower edge

Small tassels enliven the points on an inverted pleat tab valance

Piping and tassels accent a solid border on a patterned valance

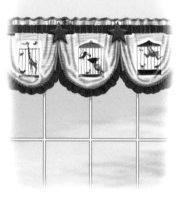

Sprightly stuffed cloth stars trim a colorful cloud valance

A tailored bow with long tails over an inverted pleat

A lace swag finished with a big pouf knot softens a flat valance

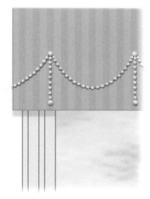

Strings of beads form a swag-and-dangle pattern across a flat valance

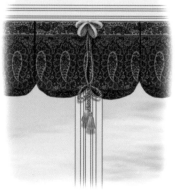

Bows of ribbon and tasseled cord on a balloon valance

Simple knots tied in cord and strategically placed on box pleats

A fringe of crisscrossed tape and balls on a plain flat valance

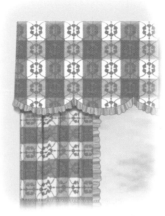

A very petite ruffle on a scalloped hemline

A diminutive, pleated ruffle on a boldly pleated valance

A soft double ruffle with a contrasting layer on a shaped hemline

An eclectic fringe of individually attached feathers

A soft, informal edging of simple scalloped fringe

An airy flourish of tassel fringe on braid on a deep scalloped valance

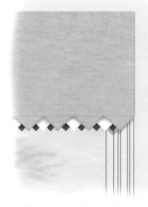

A tailored, graphic border of overlapping triangles

Cord used to secure and frame the top of a gathered valance

pleated valances

A PLEATED VALANCE gives a tailored finish to a window, especially if used over floor-length panels.

When you make the pleats and the spaces between them the same size, you create a classic box-pleated valance. If the pleats are more widely spaced, it's called a kick-pleated valance. Construction is basically the same for both types.

PLANNING

Pleated valances are board-mounted; see the hardware information on page 96 for the board sizes. The return size is equal to the width of the board.

It's best to hide seams within the pleats. To do this, before buying fabric, you must sketch your design and refer to the following directions to see how to cut and piece the widths to ensure each seam falls inside a pleat. If you're using fabric with a vertical stripe or large horizontal repeat, you may need extra yardage and more seams to keep the pattern positioned nicely on the visible spaces between the pleats.

Start by choosing space and pleat sizes. A good pleat width is 6 inches (12 inches before being pleated); space width can vary from 6 inches, for a classic box-pleated valance, up to the usable width of the fabric less the pleat size, for a kick-pleated one. You may also combine box and kick pleats, as on the drawing above.

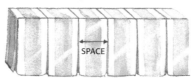

BOX-PLEATED VALANCE

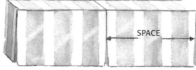

KICK-PLEATED VALANCE

Full pleats are usually placed at each corner, with half the pleat on the front and half on the return. If your return is less than half a pleat deep, place a half-pleat, rather than a full one, at each end.

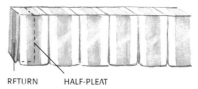

RETURN   HALF-PLEAT

See the valance guidelines on page 96 to choose the finished length, with the following considerations: On a box-pleated valance, the width of the spaces should be less than the finished length of the valance; otherwise, the spaces will appear too square. On a kick-pleated valance, the spaces will be much wider than the valance length because the pleats are fewer and farther apart.

Once you decide on pleat and space sizes, make a sketch of your valance. For a classic box-pleated style, start adding up pleats and spaces from one end of the valance, beginning with the 1¼-inch side hem and the return. The first seam will occur at the point where you reach your usable-width figure (52 inches in this example). If you're lucky, the seam will fall within a pleat and be hidden.

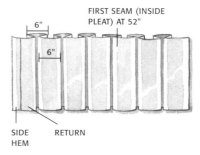

FIRST SEAM (INSIDE PLEAT) AT 52"

6"   6"

SIDE HEM   RETURN

If the seam falls in a space, back up and plan to join widths so the seam falls within the previous pleat.

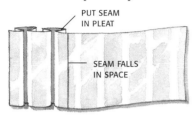

PUT SEAM IN PLEAT

SEAM FALLS IN SPACE

Continue adding spaces and pleats, adjusting seams as necessary and noting their positions on your sketch so you can cut the fabric to the needed widths and join them accurately.

For a kick-pleated valance, follow the same approach. If a seam falls in the first space, you'll need to split a width and seam half to the left side. Shift the fabric to make that seam fall in the first pleat.

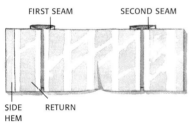

FIRST SEAM   SECOND SEAM

SIDE   RETURN
HEM

CHOOSING FABRIC

Select fabric with enough body both to form a crisp pleat and to hold its shape in the space between pleats.

It's easiest to use an unpatterned fabric for a pleated valance. With patterned fabric, choose a space size that allows the major motifs to be centered in the spaces. Make sure there's enough fabric between the horizontal repeats to make the pleats.

great pleat variations

Interesting effects can be achieved by varying the pleat spacing, adding curves to the bottom of spaces, forming box pleats on the face of the valance, double- or triple-stacking the pleats, or adding tails to the returns. The names for the variations shown are common, but not universal.

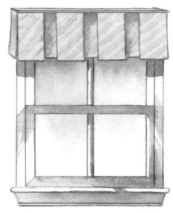

Saxony: spaced box pleats on face

Palais: stacked box pleats on face

Benton: characterized by spaces with a curved hemline

Canterbury: stacked box pleats on the face, top pleat curved at hem

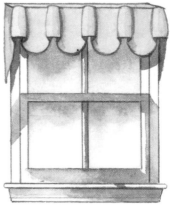

Imperial: spaced box pleats on the face with deeply scalloped spaces and pointed tails on the returns

pleated valances

CALCULATING YARDAGE
For either valance, follow these steps:

1 Measure your window and fill in the window treatment work sheet (see pages 14–18) to arrive at board size.

2 Divide the space size into the board size to arrive at the number of spaces. If the result is a fraction, round off to a whole number.

3 Divide number of spaces into board size to get exact space size.

4 Add returns to board size to get finished width.

5 Instead of filling in fullness on work sheet, multiply pleat size by number of pleats (one more than number of spaces; if a half-pleat is at each corner, the number of pleats and spaces is the same). Add this figure to finished width. Add side hems for total width. Divide by usable width; round up to next whole number for number of widths needed. Add one width to compensate for adjustments.

Use the following allowances in your calculations:

	FABRIC	LINING
LOWER HEMS	3"	1¹/₂"
SIDE HEMS	5"	NONE
TOP	3"	3"

PLEATED VALANCES STEP-BY-STEP

1 Choose and prepare face fabric and lining (see pages 21–26). Join fabric widths, trimming as planned to conceal seams. (Measurements on step 4 sketch assume seaming is complete). Press seams open.

2 Follow step 2, "Rod-pocket valance," page 97, to stitch the lower hem.

3 On right side of face fabric, measure from lower edge a distance equal to finished length and mark with a fabric marker across valance. Measure and mark 3 inches above finished-length line on face fabric and lining. Trim ravel allowance.

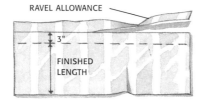

4 With face fabric right side up, measure 2¹/₂ inches on each side for hem and then measure depth of return; mark total with a pin placed vertically on finished-length line and on lower edge. At one end, measure from these pins and pin again to mark first pleat (12 inches for full pleat in example) and first space (6 inches in example).

Continue measuring and pinning pleats and spaces across valance, making sure seams fall within pleats. Last pleat should fall just before marked return.

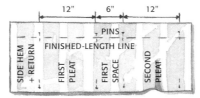

5 Bring pins together so pleats form a flattened loop on back and folds "kiss" on front.

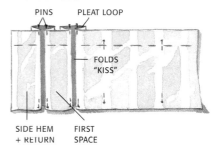

On front and back, pin layers together where pleats fold.

6 For side hems, turn face fabric 2¹/₂ inches to the wrong side and press. Turn raw edge in to meet pressed fold and press again. Fold corners diagonally to form miter (see page 28). Blindhem by machine or hand-slipstitch hem to lining only.

7 Follow first part of step 15, "Flat Roman shade," page 77, to cover mounting board.

8 On right side of valance, measure and cut top allowance ¹/₄ inch less than width of board. Fold along finished-length line and press. Also press pleats in place above finished-length line. Serge or zigzag the top raw edge, joining face fabric and lining.

9 Position valance right side up over board so finished-length fold aligns with top front edge of board and pleats are at corners. Staple top allowance to board; fold and staple returns.

10 Follow directions for an outside mount in step 21, "Flat Roman shade," page 77, to install valance. On a wide window, support with angle irons every 40 inches.

bandanna valance

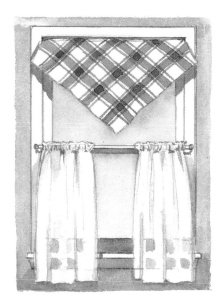

THIS EASY-TO-MAKE valance, also called a handkerchief valance, is a square or diamond shape lined to the edge in the same or contrasting fabric and attached to a rod by means of a hidden rod pocket. For a fun look, use plaid or bordered tablecloths or large bandannas instead of fabric yardage.

PLANNING

This valance can be made with a longer front triangle that hides the back one or reversed so that the edges of the longer back triangle accent the shorter one in front. The placement of the off-center rod pocket determines the look and allows the ends of the valance to hang in short tails.

The best rod to use is a 1³/₈-inch-diameter pole, with or without finials.

The length of the valance is optional, depending on the look you want. The wider the window and the squarer the flat valance, the more window is covered.

The width of the valance is from tail point to tail point.

It's smart to make a mockup so you can check the proportions.

CALCULATING YARDAGE

Measure your window and fill in the window treatment work sheet (see pages 14–18). The width from point to point is the bracket-to-bracket measurement plus at least 8 inches (4-inch tails on each side). If your valance will be cut with its length on the lengthwise grain of your fabric, the maximum width from bracket to bracket is 42 inches. If cut on the bias, the maxium width, including ¹/₂-inch seam allowances on all sides, is the bias of your fabric. The length from point to point is twice the distance from the top of the rod to the longer bottom point minus 3 inches.

BANDANNA VALANCE STEP-BY-STEP

1 Make a paper pattern for one-half of the length of the finished valance. Draw a horizontal line the total width of the valance at the center. From the center point of the horizontal line, draw a vertical line for one-half of the finished length of the valance. Draw diagonal lines joining the two end points to the bottom of the vertical line. Add ¹/₂-inch seam allowance to the diagonal edges. Cut out the pattern.

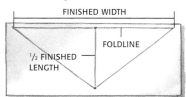

2 Use the pattern to cut one piece of face fabric and one of lining; be sure to reverse the pattern on the finished-width line to cut a complete diamond. Place the face fabric and lining right sides together with edges aligned.

3 Using ¹/₂-inch seam allowance, stitch all around; leave an opening for turning. Trim corners, turn right side out, and press. Slipstitch opening.

4 With a chalk marker, draw center horizontal line on lining. Measure and mark 1¹/₂ inches to one side of center line and draw a parallel line.

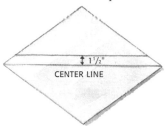

5 Cut a strip of lining fabric the length of the bracket-to-bracket measurement and wide enough to form a rod pocket (see page 53) plus 1 inch. Press under ¹/₂-inch seam allowances on all edges of strip.

6 Place strip on lining side of valance, aligning one edge on point side of second horizontal line; trim strip if it extends past diamond. Edgestitch both long sides, leaving ends open.

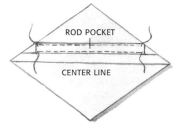

7 Slip a rod into the rod pocket. Mount rod in the brackets.

cornices

ABOVE: *A tall proportion and double-scalloped lower edge give a traditional elegance to this cornice, which is covered in a simple allover pattern that picks up the drapery color below.*

RIGHT: *Shirred fabric secured at top and bottom with a self-fabric welt adds subtle texture to a plain cornice—effectively paired with this sheer stripe Roman shade.*

OPPOSITE: *Tailored and timeless, this straight cornice is upholstered with the fabric used for the draperies and edged with wood molding.*

how to make cornices

A FABRIC-COVERED wood cornice mounted over curtains, draperies, or a shade neatly frames a window and adds architectural interest to a room. A cornice is practical, too—it hides the heading and the hardware at the top of the undertreatment.

You make a scalloped cornice in much the same way that you make a straight cornice; where steps differ, special instructions for the scalloped version are given.

tools and supplies

To make a straight or scalloped welted cornice, you will need the following supplies from a lumberyard: 1-inch No. 2 kiln-dried pine for the top and legs (the width and length depend on the dimensions of your cornice) and 3/8-inch interior fir plywood for the face (the amount depends on the cornice dimensions).

You'll need a saber saw or handsaw, cement-coated box nails, paper for pattern (for scalloped cornice only), white or craft glue, a paintbrush, scissors, C-clamps, a staple gun, angle irons, and fasteners.

Additional supplies include 8-ounce bonded Dacron batting (to wrap around legs and face board); pushpins; fabric for the cornice, welt, and lining; upholstery tack strips; 3/8-inch cord; and gimp.

planning your cornice

Measure the width of your window from trim to trim. Then decide how far to extend the cornice on either side. The top board must be at least 1 1/2 inches longer than the window width or the treatment to be covered.

The width (front to back) of the top board depends on what will hang underneath. Over an inside-mounted treatment, such as miniblinds, the top board can be 3 1/2 inches wide. Over an outside-mounted treatment, make the top board at least 5 1/2 inches wide.

The width (top to bottom) of the face board is the desired height of the cornice; it must be the same length as the top board. The rule of thumb is for the top of the cornice to be at least 8 inches above the window opening, and the bottom 4 inches below it, for a face board that is 12 inches tall. Make sure any vertical repeat on your fabric fits attractively on the face board.

On a scalloped cornice, allow a difference of at least 3 inches between the shortest and longest points. The short points must cover the heading of any undertreatment.

The boards that form the legs are the same width as the top board. Their length is equal to the desired height of the cornice minus 3/4 inch.

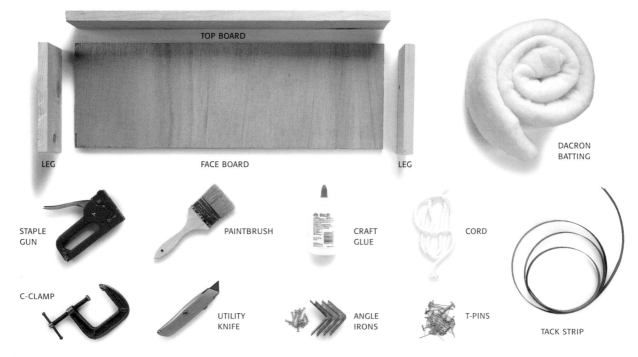

TOP BOARD

LEG   FACE BOARD   LEG

DACRON BATTING

STAPLE GUN   PAINTBRUSH   CRAFT GLUE   CORD

C-CLAMP   UTILITY KNIFE   ANGLE IRONS   T-PINS   TACK STRIP

The tools and supplies necessary for making a cornice are available in a variety of places: lumberyards, hardware stores, craft supply stores, and outlets for sewing supplies.

great cornice ideas

Cornices are easy to embellish: You can add moldings, trimmings, a skirt (make it like a valance and staple it inside the cornice), or other layers of fabric. Combine embellishment and scalloped lower edge shapes for dressier décors.

A fabric-covered cornice with applied moldings and a railing for display of small objects

A tall cornice with contrasting borders and triangular overlays buttoned at the tips

A cornice with a peaked curve cut into the lower edge, trimmed with fringe

A grand wood cornice with a fringe-trimmed, box-pleated skirt

A simple wood cornice, faux-painted and decorated with metal holdback faceplates

A tall cornice with a scallop and point edge and applied contrast swags, jabots, rosettes, and tassels

cornices

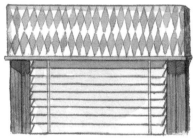

STRAIGHT

SCALLOPED

FOR A SIMPLE, tailored treatment, make a cornice with a straight lower edge. A scalloped cornice creates a softer look. Select a firmly woven fabric strong enough to be stretched taut and stapled to the cornice.

CALCULATING YARDAGE

If possible, railroad fabric (run selvages parallel to floor) to avoid seams. Most patterned fabric must be run vertically.

Add together long dimension of cornice, returns (depth of legs), and add 6 inches for wrapping around legs.

For railroaded fabric, divide by 36 inches to get yards needed (fabric width will cover cornice height).

For fabric run vertically, divide by usable fabric width for number of widths needed. The cut length is equal to the height of the cornice plus 6 inches. To figure repeat cut length for patterned fabric, see page 18. Multiply cut length (or repeat cut length) by number of widths; divide by 36 inches for yards needed.

Railroad the lining, figuring it as you would face fabric.

Add extra fabric for same-fabric or contrast welt (see step 15, page 115, to determine the length).

CORNICES STEP-BY-STEP

1 Using 1-by lumber for top board and legs and plywood for face board, measure and cut boards to your specifications. Make cuts precise; ends of all boards must be perfectly square.

TOP BOARD

FACE BOARD

LEG   LEG

2 *For a straight cornice*, continue to step 3. *For a scalloped* cornice, make a paper pattern, using a sheet of paper equal to half the long dimension of cornice and deep enough to span the short and long points.

Draw half of design, cut out, and tape to face board. Mark outline; flip pattern and mark other half. Cut face board on marked line.

3 Lay out the boards. Start nails for legs at ends of top board. Glue legs to underside of board at ends; finish nailing. Apply glue to front edge of top board and legs. Lay face board over frame.

Using nails, tack face board to top board at corners; tack to legs, pulling legs out to straighten, if necessary. Finish nailing. Measure and mark vertical line at midpoint on face board.

4 Lay cornice, face board up, on sawhorses. On batting, mark midpoint at top and bottom. Dilute glue with water to consistency of heavy cream and brush onto face board. Lay batting on top, aligning marks on board and batting. Let dry.

5 Brush glue on legs; wrap batting around legs, securing on inside of legs with pushpins until glue is dry. Trim batting even with the top, lower, and back edges.

6 *For fabric run vertically*, join widths, as described on page 26; press seams toward center. To avoid a center seam on an even number of widths, cut off half a width and seam to opposite side.

7 Center fabric, right side up, on face board to check alignment of pattern. Smooth over top board; fabric should extend 3 inches beyond top front edge. Adjust or measure, mark, and recut as needed. Remove fabric.

8 Hang cornice, top board up, over sawhorses. On top board, measure and mark a line 2 inches from front edge.

9 Center fabric, wrong side up, on top board so edge of fabric is at marked line and fabric is toward back (open edge). Starting at midpoint of top board, lay a tack strip over fabric, aligning edge with raw edge of fabric. Staple strip.

Continue stapling, placing staples 3½ inches apart and adding strips as needed, to within 1 inch of ends of cornice; trim ends.

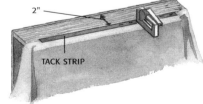

2"

TACK STRIP

10 Flip fabric forward; if any staple has pulled a thread, remove and restaple. Smooth fabric down face board and up underneath. Roll cornice back so top board is down. Clamp to sawhorses.

11 *On a straight cornice*, pull fabric taut at midpoint of face board and, keeping grain straight, wrap around bottom of face board. Staple to inside about $1^1/2$ inches from edge, placing staples about 6 inches apart. (Staples are temporary.)

On a scalloped cornice, pull fabric taut and staple at longest point or points. (Staples are temporary.)

For either cornice, pull fabric around legs and staple to inside in several places.

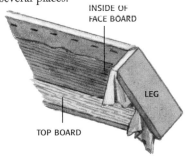

INSIDE OF FACE BOARD
LEG
TOP BOARD

12 Starting at midpoint of face board on a straight cornice or at long points on a scalloped cornice, remove a temporary staple. Pull fabric taut enough to see edge of board, and staple about $1^1/2$ inches from edge.

On a straight cornice, continue removing temporary staples, one at a time, pulling fabric taut, and restapling; keep grain straight and place staples about $1/2$ inch apart. Staple to within 4 inches of ends.

On a scalloped cornice, remove temporary staples, one at a time, pull fabric taut, and restaple. Cut into fabric at curves almost to front edge of face board. Pull each flap of fabric taut and staple to inside. If curve meets a straight edge, fold fabric carefully and staple.

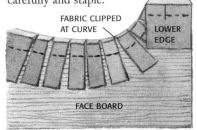

FABRIC CLIPPED AT CURVE
LOWER EDGE
FACE BOARD

13 Restaple legs in same manner, stapling fabric to inside. Roll cornice so top board is up. Fold fabric at top corners, forming miters; staple to top board. Trim close to staples.

14 Roll cornice so top board is down. At corners, cut fabric flush with inside corner; staple up to inside corners.

Smooth fabric on outside of legs, across bottom, and to inside. At corners and back of legs, neatly fold fabric under; staple to inside. Trim fabric on inside of face board and legs close to staples.

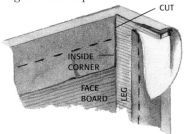

CUT
INSIDE CORNER
FACE BOARD
LEG

15 Measure, mark, and cut enough 6-inch-wide strips of bias fabric to cover lower edge of face board and legs and, if making same-fabric welt, to extend up back edge of each leg, plus 2 inches for each end plus 6 inches for each seam. Sew strips together; trim seam allowances and press open.

Lay cord on wrong side of strip. Fold strip over cord, making one seam allowance $1^1/2$ inches wider than the other. Stitch close to cord.

16 Starting at one end of face board and leaving enough welt to edge adjoining leg and, for same-fabric welt, back of leg, lay welt on front edge of face board with cord toward front and narrower seam allowance underneath. Trim tack strips to $3/8$ inch. Miter one end of a tack strip.

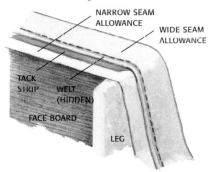

NARROW SEAM ALLOWANCE
WIDE SEAM ALLOWANCE
TACK STRIP
WELT (HIDDEN)
FACE BOARD
LEG

Lift wider seam allowance, lay tack strip on narrower allowance, against welt stitching; at same time, gently pull on bottom seam allowance so stitching is drawn slightly under strip.

17 Staple tack strip to edge of face board, placing staples about 1 inch apart and adding strips as needed. *For a scalloped cornice*, clip welt seam allowances to within $1/2$ inch of welt stitching and stretch welt slightly around curves.

At opposite corner, miter tack strip.

18 Miter a tack strip; use to staple welt to bottom of leg. Flatten and staple excess fabric in corner.

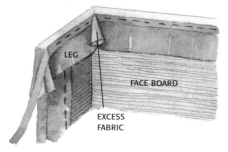

For same-fabric welt, continue stapling strip and welt up back of leg; trim strip even with edge.

For contrast welt, trim strip at back corner of leg. Repeat on other leg.

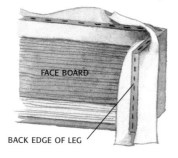

Trim narrower welt seam allowance.

19 Roll cornice so top board is up. Cut welt $1^1/2$ inches beyond end of tack strip. Rip out stitching and cut cord even with top board.

For same-fabric welt, fold fabric strip and staple to top board.

For contrast welt, fold strip and staple to inside of leg.

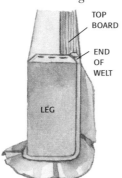

20 Roll cornice so top board is down. Starting on face board, gently pull wider welt seam allowance to inside and staple just below previous staples, placing staples 1 inch apart.

At inside corners, cut into seam allowance as before, forming a fabric flap. Miter seam allowance at back edge of leg and staple. Fold fabric flap down and staple to inside corner.

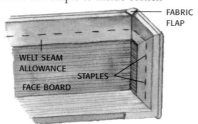

21 Roll cornice so top board is up. Center lining over top board with fabric toward front and raw edge of lining aligned with front edge of first tack strip (hidden). Lay another strip on lining so edge of strip is snug against the first strip. Staple strip; trim ends.

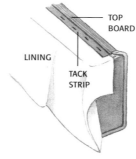

22 Flip lining to back and trim even with each end of top board. At back edge, cut lining at an angle; then turn under edge of lining and staple to top board.

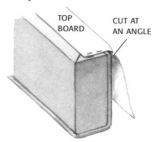

23 Roll cornice so top board is down. Smooth lining to inside and staple long edge where top board meets face board. At inside leg, fold lining over itself and cut $1/2$ inch beyond where leg meets top board; fold lining under and staple to underside of top board.

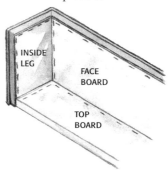

24 Staple inside edge where face board meets leg. Smooth fabric over inside of leg. Trim remaining flap of fabric to $1/2$ inch; turn under and staple to inside of leg.

25 Trim lining 1 inch beyond back edge of leg; turn under and staple leg. Repeat on other leg.

26 Staple lining to lower edge of cornice, just above previous staples. Trim close to staples. Glue gimp over raw edges.

27 Follow directions for an outside mount in step 20, "Flat Roman shade," page 77, to install cornice. On a wide window, support with angle irons every 40 inches.

plain and fancy surface finishes

Readymade cornices are available in a variety of profiles. There are rigid foam models with crevices for tuck-in upholstery and wood ones ready to finish with paint or stain. Here are some finishing ideas.

Three fabrics tucked into a foam cornice form with a capital profile

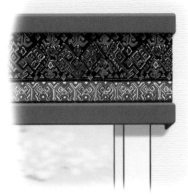

One plain and one border-print fabric tucked into a foam cornice form with square-edge top and bottom moldings

Two fabrics tucked into a foam cornice form with a gently rounded middle section

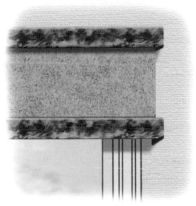

A sponge-painted wood cornice with faux tortoise-shell moldings

A wood cornice painted in faux malachite, with solid color moldings

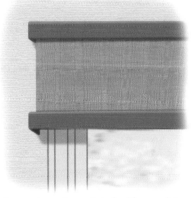

A wood cornice painted with a moiré combing technique

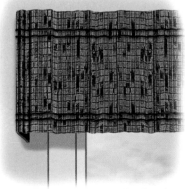

Split bamboo placemats glued to the surface of a plain cornice

A cornice covered in cork for easy picture display

swags and cascades

RIGHT: *These traditional swags have been given an informal twist—they are sewn to rings and hung from a pole instead of being stapled to a board.*

BELOW: *Plain, solid-color fabric works well for a floor-length running swag. It is understated yet effective; and there is no problem with the fabric pattern changing orientation as it travels up one side, across, and down the other.*

swags and cascades

RIGHT: *Floor-length running swags made in fabric that matches the walls give a soft, subtle finish. They're easily adapted for different size windows. Plus, if they puddle on the floor, your math doesn't need to be perfect.*

BELOW: *Common coat hooks affixed above the window provide support for this quirky swag, which is just a length of sheer fabric cleverly draped to form a large scallop and short tails.*

RIGHT: *This cutout swag with cascades is less formal than the same style hung over long draperies and it's nicely proportioned for its location.*

OPPOSITE: *The stripes are vertical on all pieces of this fringe-trimmed, formal cutout swag and cascades—an effect that's not possible with a running swag.*

swags and cascades

BELOW: *Two small swags raised at the center and topped with a Maltese cross look prim, proper, and not at all fussy in plain white. The cascades that flank them return to the wall. Be sure to make a mockup to test this swag shape.*

TOP RIGHT: *Traditional swags and cascades over matching draperies and sheers are a classic choice for formal décor. Here, the middle swag is made from the same contrasting fabric as the cascade lining.*

RIGHT: *A running swag with short tails is a soft and very easy alternative to a valance. This one is hung in swag holders and stretched taut across the top of the window.*

Traditional swags need not be limited to dressy or formal interiors. These are made in muslin and hung informally behind rod-sleeve valances that cover their tops with a soft ruffle.

how to make swags and cascades

WHETHER casual or formal, swags and cascades impart a look of timeless beauty. Some styles are simple to make; others are more difficult.

Swags are draped top treatments that are board-mounted, placed in swag holders, or wrapped around a pole. They're almost always paired with cascades and often top curtains or draperies as well.

Traditional, closed-top swags possess a simplicity that belies their construction. They appear to be nonchalantly draped over boards but are, in fact, structured and precisely made. Closely related are cutout swags, which are similarly draped but are U-shaped at the top.

Cascades are pleated side panels that flank traditional or cutout swags. Because all lines are straight, they're simple to make.

If you like the look of swags and cascades but prefer an easier project, consider a running swag. Made from one length of fabric and draped over holders or wrapped around a pole, running swags are informal yet still sophisticated.

Rosettes, cockades, and choux (see pages 136–138) are flowerlike fabric embellishments used to trim swags.

swag hardware

Traditional swags and cascades are mounted on boards. For swags used with cascades, a 3½-inch board is best. For swags used over additional treatments, choose a board that will clear both the heading and the hardware beneath it.

Use hook-and-loop fastener tape to attach cutout swags to decorative rods. A decorative traverse rod without the rings works well; the flat back on these rods makes it easy to attach the tape. Or attach the fastener tape to a pole 1⅜ inches or larger in diameter.

Running swags can hang from decorative poles, tulip-shaped or circular swag holders, medallion or scarf swag holders, or swag rings. Running swags with knots or ties are mounted on boards.

Many holdbacks (see page 51) also work as swag holders.

choosing fabric

Since a successful swag depends on the fabric's draping qualities, make sure your fabric is soft enough to drape yet firm enough to form and retain folds.

To test a fabric's draping qualities, unroll several yards and fold the cut edge to one selvage. Grasp diagonally opposite corners and hold the fabric up to see how the fold falls. If it drapes nicely, the fabric will make softly rounded swags. If the fold breaks rather than drapes, you can still use the fabric, but you'll have to work harder to form the pleats. If a fabric doesn't have enough body, an interlining may provide the right heft.

Some running swags can be made from firmly woven fabrics, such as chintz, since the hardware determines the swag's form. Wrapped swags lend themselves to soft fabrics. For both, avoid fabrics with obvious one-way patterns because the cascades will run in opposite directions.

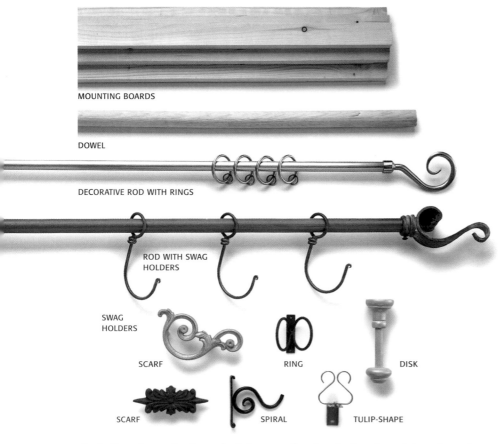

MOUNTING BOARDS

DOWEL

DECORATIVE ROD WITH RINGS

ROD WITH SWAG HOLDERS

SWAG HOLDERS

SCARF

RING

DISK

SCARF

SPIRAL

TULIP-SHAPE

A selection of swag hardware includes mounting boards, dowels, curtain rods, and swag holders in interesting shapes to coordinate with any decor.

traditional swags and cascades

MAKING BEAUTIFUL swags takes time, as well as some creativity. Before you commit to yards of fabric, make a sample swag using the fabric and lining you like to get a feel for how swags are made and what they'll look like. Use the sample to calculate yardage too.

The swags and cascades in this project are pleated; directions are also given for a version with soft gathers.

PLANNING TRADITIONAL SWAGS

A swag starts with a square of fabric 6 inches larger than the desired finished width, which can range from 36 to 48 inches, depending on the width of your fabric. Length varies; in general, it will be about one-third the size of the fabric square.

Swags can be used singly or in a series; the number depends on both board size and swag size. Swags often overlap by half the swag width, an arrangement called a classic swag. Swags can also meet, or "kiss."

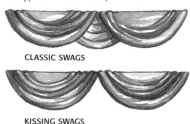

CLASSIC SWAGS

KISSING SWAGS

Swags are usually installed 8 inches above the top of the window opening or at ceiling height. The point where the swags cross should be 2 to 4 inches into the window area.

Typically, swags used with cascades extend 4 to 6 inches beyond each side of the opening, with a portion of each cascade covering the window. If you're planning tied-back side panels, place half the panel on the window. For straight panels, place most of each panel off the window. Plan a swag treatment as follows:

1 Measure your window width and add extensions (see page 14) to arrive at board size. (In example, the board size is 90 inches.)

2 *For swags that meet,* divide board size by 40 inches (a trial swag width) and round up to next whole number to arrive at number of swags (90 ÷ 40 = 2.25; rounds up to 3). *For overlapping swags,* multiply the board size by $1^1/2$, divide by 40, and round up to next whole number ($90 \times 1^1/2 = 135 \div 40 = 3.38$; rounds up to 4).

3 Sketch your arrangement, showing full swags and half-swags, if swags overlap. Add number of full and half-swags that you see (1 full swag + 3 half-swags = $2^1/2$).

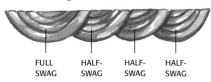

FULL SWAG   HALF-SWAG   HALF-SWAG   HALF-SWAG

4 Divide board size by result in step 3 for actual swag width in inches (90 ÷ $2^1/2$ = 36). Count the number of swags needed—you must make a full swag even if only half shows.

CALCULATING YARDAGE

Add 6 inches to the actual finished width to arrive at the cut length of each square. For patterned fabric, figure the repeat cut length following steps 2–3 on page 18. For a single swag, cut only one length; for more than one swag, multiply the cut length or repeat cut length by the number of swags.

Use lining the same width as your fabric; buy the same amount.

SWAG TIPS

When pleating your swag, have a helper stand on the other side of your work area. Otherwise, make and pin pleats one at a time on each side. Either way, you'll need to make adjustments to achieve uniformly rounded folds.

Mark the finished width on your ironing board cover and pin the swag to one edge to see how it hangs.

TRADITIONAL SWAGS STEP-BY-STEP

1 Choose and prepare face fabric and lining (see pages 21–26).

2 Measure, mark, and cut a square of lining equal to finished swag width plus 6 inches (42 inches in example).

3 Fold lining in half diagonally, wrong side in, making a triangle; fold again, bringing first fold almost to side. Finger-press folds.

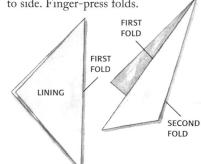

FIRST FOLD

FIRST FOLD

LINING

SECOND FOLD

4 Unfold lining, wrong side up, and mark a point on center fold 1 inch longer than side of square (43 inches in example). Also, mark points on intermediate folds ¹/₂ inch longer than side of square (42¹/₂ inches in example). Strike a curve through marks from one corner to the other.

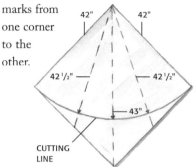

CUTTING LINE

Cut curve. If you've made a sample swag, cut linings for additional swags now, using first piece as a pattern.

5 Position face fabric right side up and determine top point of swag (make sure motifs on patterned fabric are going in right direction). Lay lining over face fabric, right sides together. If fabric is patterned, move lining until repeat is centered as desired.

Pin layers together 1 inch above curve; cut face fabric to match lining. Stitch, using ¹/₂-inch seam allowance.

6 Turn right side out. Understitch through lining and seam allowances only ¹/₈ inch from seam. Press curve, turning ¹/₈ inch of face fabric to lining side. Pin face fabric and lining together up center.

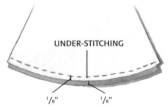

UNDER-STITCHING

¹/₈" ¹/₈"

7 With face fabric right side up, measure from top point along each side a distance equal to one-third finished swag width (12 inches in example); pin perpendicular to side. Mark a horizontal line between pins; mark a dot ³/₄ inch from edge on each side. Mark another horizontal line 3 inches below first line.

If finished swag width is 42 inches or less, add 1 inch to distance along edge below first marked line and divide by 5. *If finished swag width is 43 inches or more*, add 1 inch to distance and divide by 6. Mark edges at this increment for pleats (last pleat will be a bit smaller).

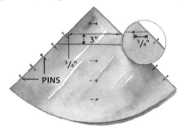

3"

³/₄"

³/₄"

PINS

8 Mark finished width line on front edge of work surface. Place swag on top, centering lower horizontal line on finished width line. Pin; let the rest hang.

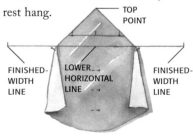

TOP POINT

FINISHED-WIDTH LINE

LOWER HORIZONTAL LINE

FINISHED-WIDTH LINE

9 On one edge, grasp fabric at second pin and, angling pleat, bring to ³/₄-inch dot; secure with a pushpin. Repeat on other side.

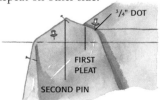

³/₄" DOT

FIRST PLEAT

SECOND PIN

10 Continue making and pinning pleats, keeping spacing even and center vertical. Form the last pleat so that the finished edge is at the ends of the finished width line.

Working from both sides, coax pleats into rounded folds; adjust and repin as necessary.

FINISHED-WIDTH LINE

FINISHED-WIDTH LINE

Pin pleats together. Check swag length; if too long, remove anchoring pushpins and move entire swag back from edge, adjusting pleats as needed.

For a gathered swag, unpin pleats, one at a time, and make small tucks; hand-stitch tucks 1¹/₂ inches from edge of work surface. Finished edge should be at the ends of the finished width lines.

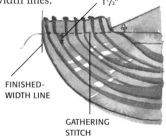

1¹/₂"

FINISHED-WIDTH LINE

GATHERING STITCH

11 Mark a line on swag parallel to and 1¹/₂ inches from edge of work surface. Place lower edge of 1-inch masking tape on marked line. Stitch on line through all layers; remove pins. Trim swag along upper edge of tape; remove tape.

1" MASKING TAPE

1¹/₂"

12 Cut a lining strip 4 inches wide by swag width; have a selvage along one long edge, or finish one edge. With right sides together, pin raw edge of strip to edge of swag. Stitch 1 inch from edge using the previous stitching as a guide.

Wrap strip over edge to the back of swag. Edgestitch through all layers.

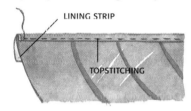

PLANNING CASCADES

Cascades can go over or under a swag. For color and pattern continuity, self-line cascades. But if you want to see another color or pattern from the front where the pleats break, line the cascades with a contrast fabric. Cut a sample cascade from lining or scrap fabric and experiment with length and pleat and space sizes before you cut your face fabric.

Traditional cascades are pleated, though you can gather them to match gathered swags. On a gathered cascade, the inside edge appears scalloped.

Length varies, depending on the look you want to achieve. As a rule, the cascade at its longest point is at least twice as long as the swag.

The steeper the taper on the lower edge, the more lining you'll see. The effect is most pleasing if the taper begins above or below the bottom of the swag, not level with it.

Each cascade is made from one width of fabric. A typical cascade has a 4-inch leading edge space, four 6-inch pleats alternating with three 2-inch spaces, and a return; finished width is 10 inches, not including the return.

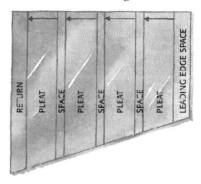

making a jabot

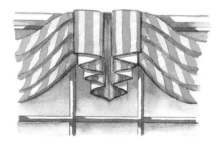

A jabot is a board-mounted decorative element used between swags. It can be short or long and is usually lined.

On a short jabot, the longest point should be shorter than the swag. Typically, the taper begins 5 to 8 inches above the longest point, pleats are 6 inches wide, spaces between pleats are 1 inch, and side spaces are 3 inches. Pleated width is 10 inches.

On a longer jabot, side taper begins at longest point of swag or below; finished length varies. Pleats are 6 inches wide, spaces between pleats are 2 inches, and side spaces are 4 inches. Pleated width is 16 inches.

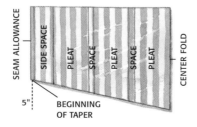

1 Cut the face fabric and lining to finished length plus 4 inches for a 1/2-inch seam allowance and an allowance to go over the top of the mounting board.

2 Place fabric and lining right sides together. Stitch all around, leaving an opening for turning. Turn right side out, press, and slipstitch closed.

3 Mark the finished-length line at the top, and mark pleats and spaces at both top and bottom edges.

4 Form pleats, working from center to outer edges and reversing fold direction on one half. Stitch pleats in place 1 inch above finished-length line. From finished-length line, stitch another line at a distance equal to width of board less 1/2 inch. Trim 1/4 inch beyond stitching.

5 Staple jabot to mounting board (usually on top of swags), aligning finished-length line with front edge.

traditional swags and cascades

For a narrower cascade, make the pleats 7 inches and the spaces 1 inch for a finished width of 7 inches.

Sketch your cascade and add up the sizes of the pleats and spaces to determine where to trim the fabric width; be sure to add a $\frac{1}{2}$-inch seam allowance on each side.

For a gathered cascade, multiply desired finished width by $2\frac{1}{2}$ and add seam allowances to arrive at cut width.

CALCULATING YARDAGE

Each cascade requires one width of fabric the desired finished length (measured at the longest point), plus 4 inches total for seam allowances and an allowance to go over the top of the mounting board.

Take into account repeats on patterned fabric: cascades look best if a full repeat is at the top, just below where the cascades break over the board. Or you can center one repeat on the cascade, splitting repeats above and below. Don't put a full repeat at the bottom—most of the design will be cut away when the cascade is tapered. Place repeats at the same level on cascades; they won't be mirror images of each other, but the arrangement of the color will be the same.

If your fabric doesn't have a directional pattern and you're making self-lined cascades, you can save fabric by cutting cascades as shown below. You can use the lower portion of fabric to line the opposite cascade.

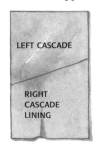
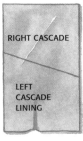

LEFT CASCADE   RIGHT CASCADE

RIGHT CASCADE LINING   LEFT CASCADE LINING

CASCADES STEP-BY-STEP

1 Lay lining and face fabric right sides together; trim to finished flat width plus 1 inch. On leading edge of each cascade, measure and mark from top a distance equal to start of taper plus 4 inches. Draw a line from the mark to the opposite lower corner. Cut on line.

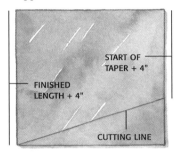

START OF TAPER + 4"

FINISHED LENGTH + 4"

CUTTING LINE

2 Pin lining and face fabric together on all edges except top. Stitch, using $\frac{1}{2}$-inch seam allowance; trim seam allowances at corners. Turn right side out; press edges.

3 Lay cascade on work surface with face fabric up. At return edge, measure and mark the finished-length line; extend the line across the top.

4 For a pleated cascade, measure and mark pleats and spaces with pins.

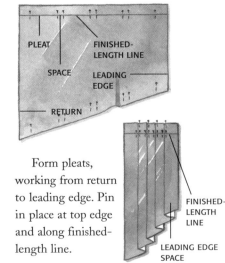

PLEAT   FINISHED-LENGTH LINE

SPACE   LEADING EDGE

RETURN

FINISHED-LENGTH LINE

LEADING EDGE SPACE

Form pleats, working from return to leading edge. Pin in place at top edge and along finished-length line.

For a gathered cascade, run a long gathering stitch by hand $1\frac{1}{2}$ inches beyond finished-length line. Gather to desired finished width.

5 With face fabric up, place lower edge of 1-inch masking tape on finished-length line. Stitch along top edge of tape. Measure $1\frac{1}{2}$ inches above stitching and mark another line; cut on line. Remove tape.

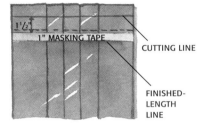

$1\frac{1}{2}$"

1" MASKING TAPE

CUTTING LINE

FINISHED-LENGTH LINE

Serge or overcast top edge, joining face fabric and lining.

MOUNTING TRADITIONAL SWAGS AND CASCADES

Staple traditional swags and cascades to a mounting board. Or, to make removal easier, use hook-and-loop fastener tape.

1 Follow first part of step 15, "Flat Roman shade," page 77, to cover mounting board.

2 Pin the cascade to the board so finished-length line is at front edge of board (first, or on top of swag if that is desired position); check length and adjust if necessary. Fold cascade at corner for return.

3 Staple cascade to board, placing staples about 2 inches apart.

4 Follow directions for an outside mount in step 20, "Flat Roman shade," page 77, to install. Support with angle irons every 40 inches.

great cascade and jabot ideas

Use cascades and jabots to add a flourish to your swags. Contrast linings, fringe or other edgings, and small changes in the proportions have great impact on their effect; here are nine ideas that are somewhat out of the ordinary.

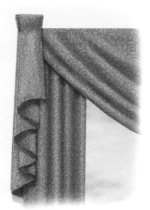

A cascade with stacked pleats and a heading

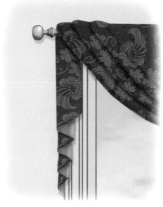

A narrow cascade with a wide top pleat and contrasting lining

A braid-edged cascade with a short inside return and contrasting lining

A large bow flopped forward over wide tails, standing in for a cascade

A flat tail with a curved lower edge (instead of a cascade) under a swag

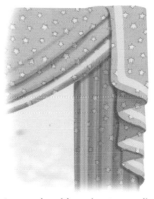

A cascade with an inset, coordinating border and top pleat with curved edge

A gathered jabot with a heading, between adjacent swags

A symmetric, crisply pleated jabot with contrast face, between adjacent swags

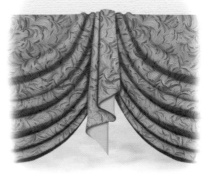

An asymmetric, softly pleated jabot between adjacent swags

cutout swags and cascades

ATTACHED TO decorative poles and often combined with sheers, miniblinds, or pleated shades, cutout swags have an open area on top so the rod shows and are visually lighter than traditional swags.

Cutout swags provide only shallow coverage for an undertreatment. If you're planning an undertreatment such as operable drapery or curtain panels, be sure to mount the swag pole high enough for the bottom of the cutout to fall above the undertreatment's heading and make sure the distance from the bottom of the cutout to the level where the swags overlap is deeper than the heading. Likewise, cutout swags usually look best if they conceal the molding and top of the window opening when used over shades or without an undertreatment.

Because of the way they're attached, cutout swags and cascades are more complex than the other swag treatments. It's helpful to make a sample first to get a feel for how the swags are made and to check the proportions. Refer to the sample to calculate yardage.

Cascades for cutout swags may return to the window or not. Directions for those with returns are on page 133.

PLANNING CUTOUT SWAGS

For guidelines in choosing fabric, see pages 21–26.

Cutout swags appear to wrap around the pole; cascades can go behind or in front of the pole. In this example, each swag is 36 inches wide, with a 16-inch cutout; the overlap is 10-inches. The cascades are behind the pole.

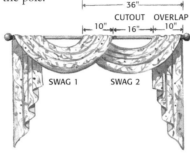

Swags start with a square of fabric 6 inches larger than the desired finished width, which can range from 32 to 48 inches, depending on your fabric's width. The cutout should be between 16 and 20 inches wide. Overlaps are from 8 to 12 inches; 10 inches is standard.

The rod or pole is usually installed 8 inches above the top of the window opening. When planning the overall width, don't forget the treatment can cover only the distance from the inside of one bracket to the inside of the other. Extensions for swags used with cascades are typically 4 to 6 inches, allowing a portion of each cascade to cover the window. If you're planning tied-back side panels rather than cascades, place half of each panel on the window and half off. For straight panels, place most of each panel off the window.

To figure the number of swags and their width, complete the following steps. If you want one more swag than this method yields, return to step 3 and refigure, using the new number of swags.

1 Measure your window width and add extensions (see page 14) to arrive at rod or pole size. (In the following example, rod or pole size, from bracket to bracket, is 62 inches.)

2 Divide rod or pole size by a trial swag size of 35 inches, and round off to nearest whole number to arrive at number of swags ($62 \div 35 = 1.8$; rounded to 2).

3 Multiply number of overlaps (one more than number of swags) by a trial overlap size of 10 inches ($3 \times 10 = 30$ inches).

4 Subtract result in step 3 from rod or pole size; divide by the number of swags to arrive at the cutout size ($62 - 30 = 32 \div 2 = 16$ inches).

If cutout size is less than 16 inches, reduce trial overlap in step 3 to 9 inches and refigure; if cutout is still less than 16 inches, reduce overlap to 8 inches and refigure. If cutout size is greater than 24 inches, increase overlap to 11 or 12 inches and refigure.

5 To cutout size, add 2 times overlap size to arrive at swag width ($16 + 20 = 36$ inches). Sketch your treatment.

CALCULATING YARDAGE

Calculate yardage for cutout swags in the same way as for traditional swags (see page 125).

SWAG TIPS

You'll need to adjust the folds until they're uniformly rounded. If you don't have a helper, make and pin the pleats one at a time on each side.

Mark the finished width on your ironing board cover and pin the swag to one edge to see how it hangs.

CUTOUT SWAGS AND CASCADES STEP-BY-STEP

1 Choose and prepare face fabric and lining (see pages 21–26).

2 Follow steps 2–4, "Traditional swags," pages 125–126, to cut lining and lower curve.

3 With lining right side up, measure and mark from top point down each side a distance equal to cutout size plus 3 inches (19 inches in example). Measure and mark from top point down center a distance equal to cutout size plus 2 inches (18 inches in example). Strike a gentle curve from side marks to center mark; cut along curve.

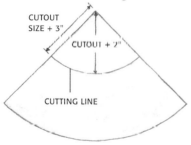

4 Position face fabric right side up and determine top of swag (make sure motifs on patterned fabric are going in right direction). Lay lining over face fabric, right sides together. If fabric is patterned, move lining until repeat is centered as desired.

Pin layers together along curves; cut face fabric to match lining. Pin and stitch lower curve only, using 1/2-inch seam allowance.

5 Follow step 6, "Traditional swags," page 126, to understitch lower curve. Do not pin along center; instead, turn inside out again. Pin and stitch upper curve, using 1/2-inch seam allowance. Turn right side out; press.

6 Measure distance along each side and divide by 5 to arrive at pleat size. If less than 5 inches, divide distance by 4. Measure pleat size incrementally along edges and mark with pins for pleat positions.

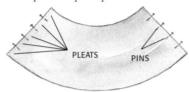

7 Use tape to mark finished swag width (36 inches in example) and midpoint (18 inches) directly on work surface or cutting board. On each side of the midpoint, mark half the cutout size (8 inches).

8 Turn under 1/2 inches along each end of upper curve. On each side, pin first pleat to work surface, angling and aligning with cutout lines. Secure the pleat with pushpins.

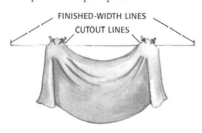

9 Continue making and pinning pleats, keeping spacing even and center vertical. Form the last pleat so that the finished edge is at the ends of the finished width line. Adjust pleats as necessary.

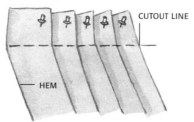

Working from both sides, coax pleats into rounded folds; adjust and repin as necessary.

Pin pleats together. Check swag length; if too long, remove anchoring pins and move entire swag back from edge, adjusting pleats as needed.

For gathered swag, unpin pleats, one at a time, and make small tucks; hand-stitch tucks 1/2 inches from edge of work surface. Finished edge should be at the ends of the finished width lines.

10 *To make cascades,* follow steps 1–4, "Cascades," page 128, disregarding references to returns. Make finished width equal to size of overlaps (10 inches in example).

11 To find total length of hook-and-loop fastener tape, multiply number of swag overlaps by 2; multiply result by size of each overlap plus 1 inch (in example, 3 × 2 = 6 × 11 = 66 inches).

12 Cut two strips of hook and-loop fastener tape equal to the overlap size plus 1 inch.

On a rod with a flat back, glue hook (stiff) strips to rod inside brackets.

On a round pole, have a helper hold pole securely on work surface. Using a board laid against pole as a guide, attach masking tape in a straight line; mark inside of brackets. Align hook strips with masking tape inside marks and glue.

For more than one swag, attach other strips at overlap positions.

13 *For a swag or cascade that goes over rod,* proceed to step 14.

For a swag or cascade that goes behind rod, measure distance from bottom of rod to top of hook strip.

cutout swags and cascades

On treatment, measure and mark finished-length line; pin perpendicular to line and baste. Measure and mark another line above finished-length line at distance just determined. Place top edge of masking tape on top line.

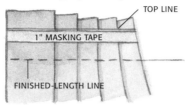

Stitch on top line; trim ¼ inch beyond stitching. Remove masking tape and basting.

14 *For a swag or cascade that goes over rod,* determine distance over rod to bottom of hook strip on back (typically 2½ to 3 inches) by having a helper hold a straightedge vertically behind rod so finished-length measurement (16 inches in example) is at top of rod. With a flexible tape measure, measure from bottom of hook strip on back of rod, up and over rod, to bottom of straightedge.

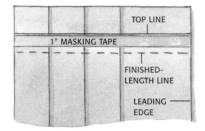

From this figure, subtract finished length of swag or cascade for margin needed above finished-length line.

On treatment, mark finished-length line; pin perpendicular to line and baste. Measure and mark another line above finished-length line at distance just determined. Place the top edge of the masking tape on top line.

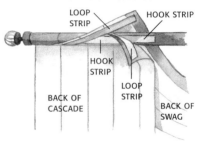

Stitch on the top line; trim ¼ inch beyond stitching. Remove masking tape and basting.

MOUNTING CUTOUT SWAGS AND CASCADES

The directions that follow are for the arrangement shown on page 130. For other arrangements, make a sketch to plan the order of attachment; overlap the elements to look like a continuous piece of fabric. Always attach the swags or cascades that go behind the rod before those that go over the rod. A helpful hint in determining which strip to use: hook strips face the wall; loop strips face the room.

1 Install the rod or pole (see pages 39 and 63).

2 On front of each cascade, sew a loop strip, aligning top of strip with top row of stitching. On back, sew a hook strip.

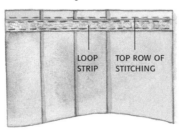

3 On outer overlaps of swags 1 and 2, which go over rod, sew a loop strip to back, aligning the top of strip with row of stitching. Repeat at the center overlap of swag 1.

4 On center overlap of swag 2, which goes behind rod, sew a loop strip to front of swag and a hook strip to back.

5 Attach the cascades to the rod. At the ends, place the swags over the rod and attach to the cascades.

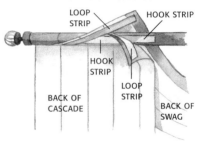

6 At center, attach swag 2 behind the rod; lift swag 1 over the rod and attach it to the back of swag 2.

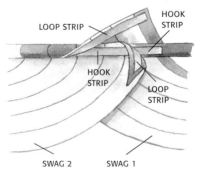

cutout swags and cascades with returns

Returns cover the gap between the wall and the side of the cascade. A notch at the top of each cascade allows the return to attach to the top of the bracket (use metal brackets).

1 Follow steps 1–9, "Cutout swags and cascades," page 131, to make swags.

2 Follow steps 1–4, "Cascades," page 128, to make cascades; return size equals distance from back of bracket to front of rod. The finished width of each cascade, not counting return, should equal size of overlaps (10 inches in example).

3 To plan notch, make two paper patterns equal to pleated width plus return. Mark return on each.

For a cascade that goes behind rod, trim pattern across top of pleated area 1 inch shorter than return portion. Where return begins, cut a V-shaped notch, extending it below top of pleated area by width of hook-and-loop fastener tape.

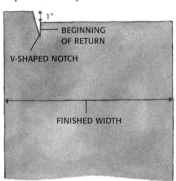

For a cascade that goes over rod, trim pattern across top edge of return area 1 inch shorter than pleated area. Where return begins, cut a J-shaped notch as deep as circumference of rod plus 2 inches and a little bit wider than the rod diameter.

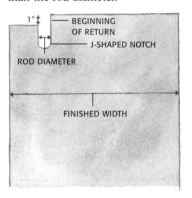

4 Follow steps 11–12, "Cutout swags and cascades," page 131, to attach fastener tape to rod.

5 *For a swag that goes behind rod,* follow step 13, "Cutout swags and cascades," pages 131–132.

For a cascade that goes behind rod, measure distance from bottom of rod to top of hook strip (typically 1 to 1¹/₂ inches). Mark this distance above the finished-length line and place top edge of masking tape along that line just up to return. On return, place top edge of tape 1 inch above that line.

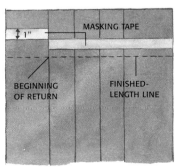

Stitch along top edges of tape; trim fabric ¼ inch beyond stitching. Trim fabric flap where return begins and remove the tape.

6 *For a swag that goes over rod,* follow step 14, "Cutout swags and cascades," page 132.

For a cascade that goes over rod, follow first two paragraphs of step 14, "Cutout swags and cascades," page 132. Measure and mark finished-length line; baste. Measure and mark another line above finished-length line at distance just determined. Place top edge of masking tape on top line.

Stitch on top line; trim ¼ inch beyond stitching. Remove tape.

Trim return portion 1 inch shorter than pleated area; serge or zigzag top edges together.

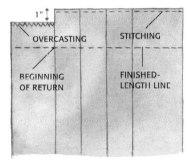

7 Using paper pattern, cut V-shaped or J-shaped notch in returns. Finish the edges; remove the basting.

8 Follow steps 1–6, "Mounting cutout swags and cascades," page 132, to mount treatments, with these additional considerations for cascades: On a cascade that goes behind rod, loop strips are attached to front of cascade and back of return; on one that goes over rod, loop strips are attached to back of cascade and return; for either, glue a hook strip to top of each bracket.

sophisticated rosettes

Rosettes, and their Maltese cross and cockade cousins, are the traditional accents for the top corner of a swag. They also work well when strategically placed atop pleats on other treatments and look good on tiebacks too. These dimensional swirls, crushed poufs, and loop assemblies may be fashioned in myriad ways—from simple X-shapes made of looped ribbon to elaborate, flowerlike constructions. See pages 136–138 for basic directions to make them.

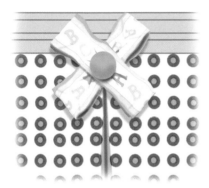

A small Maltese cross with a button center on a pleated valance

A soft Maltese cross with contrasting borders and center button

A soft Maltese cross with small choux rosette center

A Maltese cross with a small spiral rosette center, on a jabot

A Maltese cross with a choux rosette center, topping a large ruffle rosette

A soft Maltese cross with a choux rosette center and tails

A simple spiral rosette masking the holder on a scarf swag

Two fabrics rolled together to make a spiral rosette

A spiral rosette with a covered button center, on a swag with no cascade

A classic choux rosette, scaled to sit elegantly atop a gathered cascade

A loosely formed choux rosette with a smaller choux rosette center

A simple ruffle rosette with a covered button center

A large, tulle-stuffed ruffle rosette with a small choux rosette center

A choux rosette tucked into the center of a multiloop bow

A cockade of ribbon loops topped with a ruffle rosette and covered button

A large, fancy cockade with a choux rosette center, hung from a pole

making floral accents

Floral embellishments such as rosettes, choux, and cockades can be made to match or contrast with your window treatment. It's always a good idea to make a sample from muslin to check proportions before cutting your finish fabric. Pin, stitch, or glue them in place.

double ruffle rosette

To make a rosette with a rounded appearance, simply sew two ruffles out of contrast fabric and roll and stitch them together.

1 For a 6-inch, two-color rounded rosette, cut one 7-inch-wide strip from one fabric and one 6$^1/_2$-inch-wide strip from a second fabric. The cut length of each strip should be approximately 54 inches.

2 Fold each strip in half lengthwise, wrong side in, and press. To gather, place one end of button thread $^1/_2$ inch from lengthwise fold. Zigzag over thread, tapering for 6 inches until thread is $^1/_2$ inch from lengthwise raw edges; continue zigzagging $^1/_2$ inch from raw edge down length of strip.

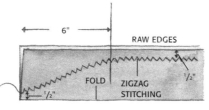

Trim excess fabric to $^1/_2$ inch from stitching at tapered end. Gather strip to approximately 22 inches for ruffle.

3 Layer the ruffles so folded edge of bottom ruffle extends $^1/_4$ inch beyond edge of top ruffle. Starting at tapered ends, begin rolling ruffles tightly; using a long needle and a thimble, stitch through gathers at base as you go.

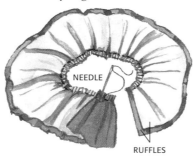

Continue rolling and stitching rosette, sewing through sides as rosette increases and folding under ends to conceal. If desired, cut and stitch a fabric circle to cover the raw edges at the center.

flat rosette

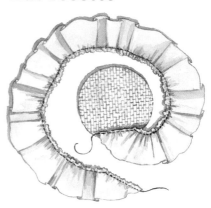

For a 4-inch rosette, cut a 3$^1/_2$-inch-wide strip and prepare it following step 2 of ruffle rosette at left. Cut a 2-inch diameter round of crinoline. Beginning with the square end of the ruffle at the perimeter, wrap and sew the ruffle to the crinoline in a spiral.

ruffled center rosette

This sweet rosette is very easy to make. You can use a strip of fabric or a piece of ribbon—it should be a little wider than the radius of the desired rosette, and 1$^1/_2$ to 2 times as long as the circumference (20 inches is the maximum length for this style). If using fabric, finish or bind the long edges before beginning.

1 Placing the stitches ½ to 1 inch from the edge, gather one long edge of the strip. Then sew the ends of the strip together to make a ring.

2 Adjust the gathers to pull up the center of the ring as tightly as possible. Hold the ring by the gathers, pinching the center together between your fingers, and hand-stitch straight through the gathers several times, rotating between stitches; secure the thread and cut off the excess.

3 Turn the rosette over so the ruffled center faces down. Steam the longer ruffle so it fans out. If it doesn't hold a nice shape, smooth the longer part over the central ruffle and bind with a rubber band. Let the rosette sit overnight, then remove the rubber band. Attach the rosette with the center ruffle facing up.

TIP
For a variation of this technique, make the ruffle strip wider and place the gathers halfway between the long edges. Pouf, fold, and tack the fullness as necessary after gathering and tacking the center. Experiment to find pleasing proportions.

cockades

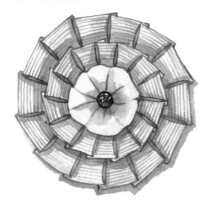

This crisp tailored embellishment is borrowed from millinery and from military uniforms. Make it from 42-inch lengths of both 1-inch- and 1½-inch-wide grosgrain or other crisp ribbon on a 4-inch square of crinoline.

1 Cut the 1½-inch-wide ribbon into fourteen 3-inch pieces. Fold each piece in half, wrong side in. String them with a hand needle onto knotted topstitching thread, piercing each through one unfolded corner about ⅛ inch inside the edges. Allow 1 inch of thread between the first strung piece and the last. Knot the thread after the last piece.

2 Join knots at the beginning and end to form a circle. Trim thread.

3 Place the ribbon circle in the center of the crinoline. Flatten the ribbons and arrange the folded petals equidistant from one another. Pin each petal to the crinoline and hand-tack in place. Trim the crinoline.

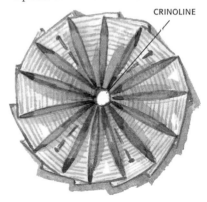

CRINOLINE

4 Repeat steps 1 and 2 using the 1-inch-wide ribbon. Pin this second ribbon circle on top of the first and hand-tack in place as in step 3.

5 Embellish the center with a small gathered fabric ruffle, making it similarly to the "Ruffled center rosette" (at left) but gathering right along the edge. Hand-tack in place, adding a decorative button for the flower center.

making floral accents

maltese cross

A Maltese cross is a double bow without tails. Depending upon your fabric choice, it will look elegant, tailored, or jaunty. Begin with strips of fabric or ribbon in a width that is a little less than half the diameter desired for the cross (for example, for a 4"-diameter cross, begin with 1½"-wide ribbon). If using fabric, finish or bind the long edges before beginning. You'll need a covered or decorative button for the center.

1 Cut two lengths of fabric or ribbon, each a little longer than twice the desired diameter of the cross. Sew the ends of each strip together to make two rings.

2 Flatten the rings into loops, centering the seam between the folded ends. Sew hand gathers across the center of each layer of one loop.

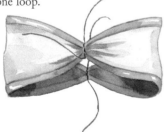

Hand-gather the center of the second loop through both layers at once.

3 Slip the second loop inside the first one at right angles and stitch together at the center. Sew the covered button over the gathers on the side without the joining seam.

choux

These decorative trimmings possess an old-fashioned charm. Choux can be made from the same or contrasting fabric; they are especially beautiful in soft silk. Start with an 11-inch square of fabric.

1 Fold the square of fabric in half diagonally, right side in. Hand-sew long running stitches along the edge of the fold, leaving a thread tail. Hand-sew long running stitches along one double-layer side of the triangle, close to the edge. Leave a tail at same point as before.

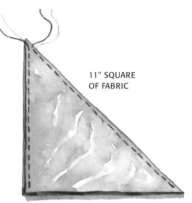

11" SQUARE OF FABRIC

2 Pin the point of the fabric with the thread tails to the center of a 6-inch square of crinoline. Pull both tails to gather the running stitches, and knot the thread tails together. Trim thread.

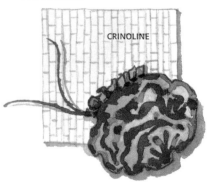

CRINOLINE

3 Turn the fabric right side out. Arrange flower on the crinoline. Steam-press lightly to set the folds. Lightly tack fabric inside the folds to retain the shape. Trim extra crinoline.

running swags

RUNNING SWAGS offer a less-structured look than traditional or cutout swags and cascades. Use them alone to frame a window or combine them with other treatments for a soft effect.

Several different styles are presented here. What makes each distinctive is the method of attachment. A running swag can be pulled through or draped over swag holders, held up by tabs or separate knots, or wrapped around a decorative rod or pole. The basic swag is the same for each style.

PLANNING RUNNING SWAGS

Running swags are made from one long piece of fabric that extends from cascade tip to cascade tip. For this treatment, the swag width is part of the cut length—when the length of fabric is turned sideways across the top of the window, the fabric width runs perpendicular to the floor in the draped area and parallel to the floor in the cascades. Directional fabric patterns are not suitable because they will invert as they travel from cascade tip to cascade tip.

The depth of the swag (from top of pole or board to bottom of drape) is up to you and depends on your fabric and window size. Do a quick mockup in muslin to see what looks good; flatten it out and use that dimension as the basis for the width of your long piece of fabric. If your fabric is very lightweight, you may want to increase the width. The depth chosen determines how many widths of fabric you need for each running swag; often you can cut two lengths from one width, using one to line the other or for a second swag.

Directions for determining the cut length accompany each project. The portion of the swag that becomes the cascades can vary from one-third to two-thirds the window length, or even extend to the floor.

If you choose asymmetrical cascades, make sure lengths differ significantly—slight variations just look like mistakes.

BASIC RUNNING SWAGS STEP-BY-STEP

1 Choose and prepare face fabric and lining (see pages 21–26).

2 Measure and cut lengths according to specific project. Cut two lengths for a self-lined swag; for a contrast lining, cut one length each of the face fabric and the contrast fabric.

3 Place fabrics right sides together. Measure in 15 inches from each end along one long edge; mark. Draw a line connecting each mark with corner on opposite edge, forming a taper. Cut along marked line through both layers.

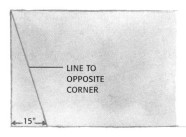

LINE TO OPPOSITE CORNER

←15"→

4 With pieces still right sides together, pin edges. Stitch all around, using ½-inch seam allowance and leaving an 8-inch opening in the middle of the longer edge. Trim allowance in points; press seams open. Turn swag right side out and press edges; slipstitch opening closed.

5 For attachment, see one of the following variations.

pouf swag

Rounded poufs accent this running treatment. You achieve the poufs, sometimes called rosettes, by pulling a basic swag through harp-shaped, tulip-shaped, or circular swag holders.

The cut length equals 1¼ times the distance between the holders, plus 30 inches for each pouf, plus 2 times the cascade length, plus 1 inch.

1 Follow steps 1–5, "Running swags," this page, to make swag.

2 Lay swag flat on work surface, lining side up, and fold accordion-style so short and long edges face in same direction. Folded swag should be about 4 inches wide.

SHORT EDGE   LONG EDGE

Using fabric scraps, tie swag loosely every 2 feet to keep folds in place.

3 Mount swag holders according to manufacturer's instructions.

4 From each end, measure finished length of cascade and slide rubber bands to this point. With shorter side facing center of window, drape swag over swag holders so rubber bands are behind holders. Remove ties.

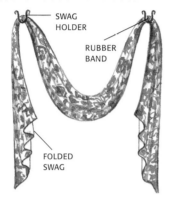

SWAG HOLDER

RUBBER BAND

FOLDED SWAG

5 From each holder, measure toward center 15 inches and mark with tape. Form a 30-inch loop so tape is at bottom of loop; place loop in holder. Remove rubber bands.

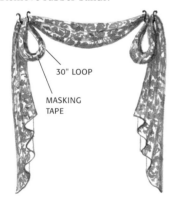

30" LOOP

MASKING TAPE

6 Adjust folds, pulling gently on the lower folds to lengthen the swag in the center and on the upper folds to keep top nearly straight.

7 To form each pouf, gently pull up the inner folds of the loop, fanning out the fabric as you pull.

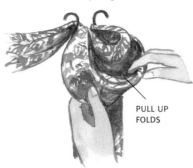

PULL UP FOLDS

Continue pulling out the folds until the pouf is full and rounded; tuck the top and bottom of the pouf back into the holder. Secure the pouf with pins. Adjust the folds in the swag and the cascades.

For two swags you will need three holders. Mark the midpoint of the swag. Measure and mark the cascades as for a single swag. Match the swag midpoint to the center holder. Measure 15 inches on each side of the midpoint for the center 30-inch loop; form the center pouf. Form the corner poufs the same way as you would for a single swag.

For three swags you will need four swag holders. Align the midpoint of the center swag with the center of the window.

scarf swag

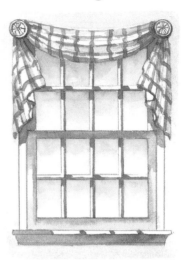

Decorative rings and medallions are designed to hold graceful scarf swags. Ring-and-pole sets hold the swag in place by means of hook-and-loop fastener tape on the back of the pole; follow the manufacturer's instructions.

The cut length equals $1\frac{1}{2}$ times the distance between holders or the pole length, plus 2 times cascade length, plus 1 inch.

1 Follow steps 1–5, "Running swags," page 139, to make swag.

2 Mount swag holders according to manufacturer's instructions.

3 Follow step 4, "Pouf swag," this page, to fold swag. Or, for a softer look, gather swag in your hands.

4 Mark midpoints on swag and window. Lay swag over holders, lining up marks. Adjust folds, pulling gently on lower folds to lengthen swag at center and on upper folds to keep top nearly straight. Adjust cascades.

tab swag and knotted swag

Though they look very different, both tab and knotted swags are mounted on a board and cradled at the corners by a band of fabric that is also stapled to the board.

With a tab swag, simple bands of fabric do the job; on a knotted swag, the bands are larger and knotted to add visual interest before they are fixed to the board.

For either style, the cut length equals the board size, plus 2 times the cascade length, plus 1 inch.

TABS

You can make self- or contrast-fabric tabs. Cut a strip of fabric 5 inches wide and 20 inches long. Fold strip lengthwise, right side in, and stitch long edges. Turn right side out, center seam at back, and press. Staple one end of the tab, seam up, to board 2 inches from the front and side.

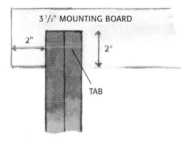

3 ½" MOUNTING BOARD

2"

2"

TAB

KNOTS

For a self-lined knot of medium-weight fabric, you need 1 yard for each knot; for sheer fabric, 48 inches. Fold fabric crosswise, right side in, and stitch cut edges together to form a tube (selvages will be at ends). For a contrast knot, you need 1/2 yard of each fabric. Stitch the two 18-inch pieces together, and then make the tube. Turn the tube right side out and tie a single knot slightly closer to one end than the other. With front end of knot down, staple long end of tube to board about 2 inches from front and side.

BOTH TABS AND KNOTS

Starting at midpoint of covered board, staple swag to board. Gather swag in your hands, forming soft pleat. Pull tabs or knots up and over swag, angling ends outward; staple and trim.

wrapped swag

This swag and cascade treatment "snakes" around the pole, forming two or more shallow swags with cascades. Single knots on each end secure the swag to the pole.

A wrapped swag can cover any window more that 36 inches wide. The cut length equals 1½ times the pole length, plus 2 times cascade length, plus 1 inch, plus the amount needed to tie knots around the pole (experiment to find length needed).

To make the swag, follow steps 1–5, "Running swags," page 139. Fold or gather the swag as in step 2, "Pouf swag," page 139.

Mark the midpoints on the swag and pole. Lining up marks, drape the swag over the pole at center, with half of the swag in front and half behind. Tie the fabric in a loose knot around the pole at each end. Adjust the folds in the swag, pulling gently on lower folds to lengthen it. Adjust the knots and cascades.

more running swags

WITH A LITTLE imagination you can drape and tie a running swag in myriad ways. For these ideas, mount the swag on a board or—even easier—if the fabric is lightweight and unlined, use thumbtacks to affix it to the top of the window molding. Basic directions are on page 139.

double drape

Use two unlined lengths of very lightweight fabric. Attach one to the top of the window. Then gather the fabric in the middle of second length into a pouf and tie some elastic around it. Place it, centered, over the first length; hold it in place temporarily with pushpins. Working with both layers as one, form poufs at the corners of the window, tying them with elastic. Remove the temporary pushpins and, if necessary, support each pouf with a hidden pushpin.

The top layer need not be as large as the bottom layer. Use lace or cotton net for one or both layers, or use contrasting-color sheers.

loop tie

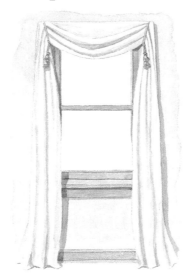

For a truly simple swag, use a tassel tieback or other decorative trim to tie up the drape. Fasten the tieback discreetly to the top of the window trim and tie it around the full width of the fabric.

multiple arc

This variation is particularly suitable for wide or multiple windows. Make a contrast band of fabric to tie in a bow around each pouf and at the center drape. Fold one band in half over the fabric edge at the top center. Attach the swag to the window (put a tack through fabric and bow strip) and tie the center bow. Then gather the fabric at each corner into a pouf and tie some elastic around it. Adjust all the drapes and tie a fabric bow around each pouf.

rosette trim

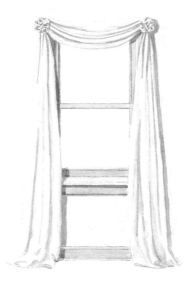

At the window corners, slip a length of narrow elastic under the fabric, wrap it around the full width, and tie. Arrange the central drape. Make coordinating rosettes (see pages 136–138) and pin or sew them over the elastic.

index

boldface numerals denote
  photographs
italic numerals denote
  techniques or project
  instructions

photography credits